WHAT'S WRONG WITH SAME-SEX MARRIAGE?

D. JAMES KENNEDY
& JERRY NEWCOMBE

CROSSWAY BOOKS

A DIVISION OF
GOOD NEWS PUBLISHERS
WHEATON, ILLINOIS

Library of Congress Cataloging-in-Publication Data
Kennedy, D. James (Dennis James), 1930-
What's wrong with same-sex marriage? / D. James Kennedy and Jerry Newcombe.
   p. cm.
   Includes bibliographical references and index.
   ISBN 1-58134-663-8 (alk. paper)
   1. Marriage—Religious aspects—Christianity. 2. Same-sex marriage. 3 Homosexuality—Religious aspects—Christianity.
I. Newcombe, Jerry. II. Title.
BV835.K4635   2004
248.4—dc22   2004013370

DP		13	12	11	10	09	08	07	06	05	04
15	14	13	12	11	10	9	8	7	6	5	4	3	2	1

WHAT'S
WRONG WITH **SAME-SEX MARRIAGE?**

This book is dedicated to
the brave men and women
who have walked out of homosexuality
by the grace of Jesus Christ,
including all those involved in Exodus International

Contents

Acknowledgments

There are a number of people to thank for this book, including our book agent Chip MacGregor of Alive Communications, and also Lane Dennis and Marvin Padgett of Crossway Books for making this possible in the first place. But also we must thank Kirsti Newcombe, who spent a great deal of time in the early editing of the manuscript. Also, we must thank my longtime secretary, the always efficient Mary Anne Bunker.

Introduction

*"You are the salt of the earth. . . . You are
the light of the world."*
MATTHEW 5:13-14

"Marriage," said Mae West, "is a wonderful institution. But who wants to live in an institution?"

All joking aside, the institution of marriage is in deep trouble in our time. Thanks to liberal court decisions, marriage is being redefined—and significantly cheapened. The state of Massachusetts is "marrying" men with men and women with women. Same-sex marriage. When you think about it, it's an oxymoron. If it's marriage, then by definition it's between a man and a woman.

This short book examines this crisis and looks at what the Bible has to say and what steps we can take to counter it. We discuss a strategy for change on two fronts: 1) conversion for homosexuals who want to change, through the power of Jesus Christ, and 2) the push for a Federal Marriage Amendment—to take such a vital issue out of the hands of activist judges.

In Part I we begin by looking at the importance of marriage and how it is being assaulted in our time—despite the amazing amount of research in its favor. Then we look at what really drives the push for same-sex marriage. What really lies behind it is homosexual activists trying to force us to accept their lifestyle whether we agree with it or not. Then we look at the issue of tolerance and intolerance. We also marshal what we see as the top twelve arguments against same-sex marriage.

Part II of the book focuses on homosexuality, its cause and cure. It is a deadly lifestyle, and those engaged in it are reaping the natural consequences of unnatural acts. Finally, we explode the myth that so much of the gay agenda is based on—that they're born that way. First, we look at what scientists and psychologists have to say on the subject. Next we look at the testimonials of ex-gays and ex-lesbians themselves.

Much of this book is politically incorrect. But it is our desire to speak the truth in love—and to help those trapped in the lifestyle to become free.

Christians are called to be the salt and light of our world. If ever America needed us to be salt and light, it is now. We owe it to our children, our grandchildren, and above all, to our Lord.

PART I

The Threat of Same-Sex Marriage

1

The Importance of Marriage

"Therefore a man shall leave his father and his mother and hold fast to his wife, and they shall become one flesh."

GENESIS 2:24

B efore the state, before the church, God created the oldest institution on this planet, and that is the institution of marriage. It is the oldest and the most universal of all of God's institutions. Wherever you would go in this world today, whatever continent, whatever nation, you would find there men and women joined together in the bonds of matrimony, rearing families.

This is a very critical time in the life of marriage. *The New York Times* declares, "The United States is becoming a post-marital society."[1] Remarkably, in the entire history of the human race, what has happened in just the last few years, a millisecond in the history of mankind,[2] is a massive effort to destroy that institution—an effort that is making ominously large strides forward.

But as far as the biblical record is concerned, God created

one man for one woman. So it was in the beginning. It's really awesome to think, ladies and gentlemen, that God took part of a man and tailor-made a woman for him. We were made for each other by divine design. So it was seen in the Old Testament, and also in the New.

Christ performed His first miracle at a wedding in Cana of Galilee (John 2). He defended marriage before the Pharisees, pointing out that when men and women departed from God's design of marriage, it was because of the hardness of their hearts. He said it was not so from the beginning. And He brought them back to creation to make His point (Matt. 19:3-9). Marriage is of historical and biblical importance, and it is basic and essential to the culture in which we live.

This nation has been built upon good families, and that has been the strength of every nation. Even Napoleon Bonaparte said that what was needed was good mothers—women in families rearing children, and with that, France would be strong, he said. He was a very perceptive man. Marriage is important for culture, it is important for individuals, it is important for husbands and wives.

But in the last few decades marriage has been under a three-fold assault, more intense than it has ever seen before. First came the *no-fault assault*, when lawyers and politicians decided they were going to make it easier to get a divorce. The result was the skyrocketing of the divorce rate in America. One recent sociologist said mountains of evidence show there never was a law passed that brought so much misery and unhappiness to so many people as no-fault divorce. Some of you have probably been through that. It has been, indeed, tragic.

Many people I have talked to have told me, "We just don't love each other anymore. Things have gotten so bad, we can't go on. We just have to get a divorce. After all, didn't we get married just to be happy?" And with that self-centered, self-indulgent, hedonistic view, which we find so prevalent today, it seems perfectly logical to get divorced. "I am not happy now. If I get a divorce, I am going to be happy in the future."

Like all of the lies of Satan, eventually time proved this idea to be false. What have the studies shown? There have been more sociological studies on marriage and divorce and families in the last few decades than ever before—taking couples that were at the point of getting a divorce, who were about to throw it all over, throw in the towel, and these studies found that five years later only 22 percent of those who went ahead with the divorce were happy. What about those who decided to stick it out, seek help and counseling, and try to fix their marriage (which for most probably seemed hopeless)? Five years later, 86 percent said they were happy.[3] God's way is the right way. Unfortunately, only too often we discover that too late.

Studies have shown that married couples, more than divorced or single people, are generally happier. They have more wealth; they, on average, have better homes; they feel their lives are more fulfilling; and, note this, they have more fulfilling sex lives than single people, in spite of what nearly every television program is saying. God's way is the right way. A tremendous book documents all these things—*The Case for Marriage* by Linda J. Waite and Maggie Gallagher. In fact, they state:

> The scientific evidence is now overwhelming: Marriage is not just one of a wide variety of alternate family forms or intimate relations, each of which are equally good at promoting the well-being of children or adults. Marriage is not merely a private taste or a private relation; it is an important public good. As marriage weakens, the costs are borne not only by individ-

ual children or families but by all of us taxpayers, citizens, and neighbors. We all incur the costs of higher crime, welfare, education and health-care expenditures, and in reduced security for our own marriage investments. Simply as a matter of public health alone, to take just one public consequence of marriage's decline, a new campaign to reduce marriage failure is as important as the campaign to reduce smoking.[4]

Yet despite all the evidence, marriage is perceived today as out-of-date, of little consequence. Meanwhile, those who promote easy, no-fault divorce have sometimes been asked, "What about the children?" Their response? "They will bounce back." It is assumed that they are sort of like basketballs—they bounce back. Well, what have the studies shown? Sociological studies have shown that the children of divorce do worse in school. They drop out more; they make worse grades; they get into more trouble. Barbara Dafoe Whitehead, author of *Culture of Divorce*, catalogs some of the fallout on children from divorce:

> For parents, divorce is not a solo act but one that has enormous consequences for children. A mounting body of evidence from diverse and multiple sources shows that divorce has been a primary generator of new forms of inequality, disadvantage, and loss for American children. It has spawned a generation of angry and bereaved children who have a harder time learning, staying in school, and achieving at high levels . . . divorce is never merely an individual lifestyle choice without larger consequences for the society. . . . It has imposed a new set of burdens and responsibilities on the schools, contributed to the tide of fatherless juveniles filling the courts and jails, and increased the risks of unwed teen parenthood.[5]

Now keep in mind, these are averages, and I am not trying to put a guilt trip on anyone reading this book. Some of you may have been divorced when you had no power to do anything about it. You were deserted, abandoned, or whatever, and you are doing the best you can to rear your children. Some of you are doing an outstanding job. But on average, children of divorce drop out more, make worse grades, get into more trouble, are expelled from school more often, are more likely to take drugs, are more likely to drink alcohol more frequently. They commit more crimes while still in school. That is not a very high bounce, is it?

And in life itself they don't do as well either. On average they get into more crime later. They make less money. They are more unhappy. And though they despise divorce, they are more likely to get one than those who have lived in intact families.

What about the impact that marriage or divorce has on how long a person lives? You may remember a longitudinal study that was begun about eighty or ninety years ago in California by Dr. L. Terman. He examined the lives of fifteen hundred children for their entire lifetimes. It was an *eighty-year* study. You say, "That must have been a very old doctor." Well, actually he died long before the study was over. Other doctors continued where he left off. These young people called themselves "Termites," after his name, and they had contact with each other and with him.

What were the results? Well, of these fifteen hundred children, some came from broken homes, and others came from intact homes. The one thing the researchers discovered was that on average, children of broken homes lived four years less. You want to get a divorce? On average, you are hacking four years off the life of your children. "It's a personal matter between your mother and me and has nothing to do with you." Wrong; it has something very definitely to do with the child. It will shorten his or her life, on average. Indeed, this is a very important issue for children. The basic reason for marriage was that men and women might not only have their own lives fulfilled and strengthened and might grow in grace together, but also so they would provide a safe and healthy place to rear children in this world.

The second assault on marriage was the *feminist* one. You remember that, don't you? The feminists said that marriage was a jail cell, a prison for women. Movement pioneer Betty Friedan likened being a housewife to being in "a comfortable concentration camp."[6] So they abandoned marriage, and they said it was a terrible thing for women. All of their fulfillment in life was going to depend on their not getting married.

Well, as you may recall, several of the leaders and founders of that movement lived long enough to say that it was a great failure. Many of these women later were rushing, as their biological clock was ticking, to get married and to have children. They found that as important as a spreadsheet might have been in their business, babies loved back, and accounting sheets did not. The feminist movement was a disastrous attack, but a failed effort. I guess they learned to outgrow Gloria Steinem's maxim that a woman needs a man like a fish needs a bicycle. She herself got married—long after she coined that phrase.

The third and most current assault on marriage is the *homosexual* one. And this is more serious than any before it, because here people are trying to destroy the very institution of marriage, to redefine it. Throughout the entire history of the world, marriage has been a union between one man and one woman. As President Bush has said repeatedly, marriage is a union between one man and one woman in America. He hopes that it will stay that way, and efforts are being made to protect marriage. How did prominent lesbian Rosie O'Donnell react to President Bush's call for an amendment? She said: "I think the actions of the president yesterday . . . are, you know, in my opinion, the most vile and hateful words ever spoken by a single president in my opinion. I am stunned, and I am horrified."[7] For taking a stand for the traditional, time-honored definition of marriage—which has proven time and again to be the best for society—the President's words were called hateful and vile.

Well, marriage is in great need of protection. Ten years ago there was not a single nation in the world that allowed anything other than one man and one woman to wed. There are some people you just can't marry. You can't marry your sister or your mother or your daughter. You can't marry the household pet. There are some things that you just can't do, and marriage has always been a union between a man and a woman. That is the way God designed it in the very beginning.

Well, what has happened? Today three countries allow marriages between two men or two women. The first of them was the Netherlands, and then Belgium, and now, more recently, Canada. And in our own country, the Supreme Court of Massachusetts ruled that same-sex marriages should be legal. They ruled this in November 2003, and on May 17, 2004— Black Monday—a thousand couples "got married" in the Bay State. This is the dropping of a cultural bomb, the threat of which most Christians don't seem to recognize.

Same-sex marriage won't remain in Massachusetts. Already homosexuals, through their legal arms, have instituted suits on all thirty-eight of the states in America that have passed DOMA laws—Defense of Marriage Acts, and they plan to take those states to court. They are using small groups of unelected officials in the courts to overthrow an institution that has existed as long as mankind has existed. And they have been amazingly successful.

What does a homosexual marriage look like? Well, the longest term that we have available to look at is in the Netherlands. Researchers found out that the average "marriage" between two men lasts one and a half years. Furthermore, during that time, men have eight other sexual partners per year.[8] In one and a half years, that would mean that during the time of that marriage, a man has had an adulterous relationship with twelve other men. This is not something they would like to have known, but it's a fact.

Here in the United States, 75 percent of heterosexual married couples report being faithful to their vows.[9] Again, from our media you would not suppose it would be 5 percent, much less 75 percent.

The most comprehensive study on sex in America to date was the one conducted in 1992 and released in 1993 by the National Opinion Research Center, which is affiliated with the University of Chicago. It exploded many myths about sex. They found that the group presented in the media as having the "hottest sex" (young, unmarried singles) were often the group least likely to have regular sex. In contrast, "boring" married couples who were faithful to each other were the ones having sex most often and with greater satisfaction. The researchers wrote:

> Once again contradicting the common view of marriage as dull and routine, the people who reported being the most physically pleased and emotionally satisfied were the married couples. . . . The lowest rates of satisfaction were among men and women who were neither married nor living with someone—the very group thought to be having the hottest sex.[10]

The study found over and over that marriage—not fornication, not adultery—brought the greatest sexual fulfillment of all.[11] Thankfully, they also found that adultery in practice was not the norm in America.[12]

But it is interesting that gays want to marry. What is it that they really want? Is it just that they want to get married? No. A number of their leaders have said that they don't really want matrimony. Why, all the legal entanglement that involves would only take away their freedom, which is the essence of their whole lives. This idea of "'til death do us part" and monogamous relationships is utterly abominable to them.

So what do they want? Well, activist leaders have said what they want is to destroy marriage altogether. They don't want to become like us, as so many naive people think. What they want to do is make us like them and to open the door to all kinds of sexual chaos. If two men can get married, what about three or five? That is called polyamory, and many loves and group marriage and all such things as this are already in the wings and are waiting to be filed in our courts. That would produce absolute cultural chaos in this country. Mother and father, husband and wife would be old-fashioned concepts in a generation. This nation would be unrecognizable. This is the most dangerous attack on marriage that the world has ever seen!

What Can Be Done?

What *can* be done? It appears that the courts cannot be counted on to act responsibly. There are the DOMAs, the Defense of Marriage Acts, which have been passed by the legislatures of thirty-eight of our fifty states already. But these laws are vulnerable. You may recall the Supreme Court's decision to overturn a case in Texas having to do with a law stating that sodomy was a crime. That law was passed by the state legislature of Texas but was overturned by the U.S. Supreme Court with the stroke of a pen. This could easily happen to all of the DOMAs, so that marriage would not be protected in any state in the union.

What can be done? The experts say the only thing that can be done is a constitutional amendment, and there is at hand a hundred proponents and signers in the House of Representatives for the Federal Marriage Amendment. It says in effect: Marriage in the United States of America is a union between a man and a woman.

Passing a constitutional amendment is a very difficult thing. Not passing this one would be disastrous. So I hope that you will pray about it. You will certainly be hearing more about it. We at Coral Ridge Ministries have been working with all kinds of other Christian organizations to do what we can to help pass the Federal Marriage Amendment, and we will do yet more. You need to first pray about it. That is vitally important. I hope you will make it a regular matter of prayer—pray for marriage in America.

Secondly, you need to contact your congressmen and senators and tell them that you want the Federal Marriage Amendment passed because marriage is too important to be destroyed in America. We all also need to work to strengthen our own marriages, which have been weakened by the other two assaults that I have mentioned before—that by no-fault divorce and that by the feminists. And now we face the homosexual assault on marriage.

Marriage is vitally important. It was obviously felt to be so by God, who made it the first institution that He created, with His own hands. We need in our day to defend it as best we can.

We are grieved at the lengths to which ungodly people will go to attack the basic institutions, the virtues and principles upon which this nation was built. We must ask the Lord to thwart their efforts. We must be faithful to work to protect marriage and to pray that our Congress may act and that the states may confirm the Federal Marriage Amendment solidifying marriage as a union between a man and a woman.

2

The Real Reason for the Push for Same-Sex Marriage

Woe to those who call evil good, and good evil,
who put darkness for light, and light for darkness,
who put bitter for sweet, and sweet for bitter!

ISAIAH 5:20

A Catholic student at Cornell University desired to serve as an RA (resident assistant). However, he had no idea what the training would entail. He and other trainees were forced to watch hours of XXX-rated pornographic homoerotic films, while being observed by a professor. If they showed any signs of disgust or revulsion, they were forced to watch more films or they failed the orientation.[1] This sounds more like the Chinese Communists' reeducation camps than a broad-minded university education. This may be an extreme case, but it points to what we believe is the actual reason for the push for gay marriage—forced acceptance of the homosexual lifestyle, whether you agree with it or not.

What's Wrong with Same-Sex Marriage?

What is the real goal behind same-sex marriage? Since homosexuals don't live faithful lives "'til death do us part," what is it they seek by being able to walk down the aisle? They are seeking the legal recognition and approval of their lifestyle. That is the goal. Same-sex marriage is a tool to help further the goal of total acceptance of the homosexual lifestyle. And regarding such *acceptance*, they don't mean for us to leave them alone to do what they want to do, but for us—all of us—to embrace it. What makes this scary to Christians is that we stand in their way. So conflict is inevitable.

Same-Sex Marriage—"The Final Tool" of the Activists

To homosexual activists, the legalization of gay marriages is a major prize. As one of them, Andrew Sullivan, put it about a decade ago: "If nothing else were done at all, and gay marriage were legalized, 90% of the political work necessary to achieve gay and lesbian equality would have been achieved. It is ultimately the only reform that matters."[2]

Robert Knight, director of the Culture and Family Institute, a division of Concerned Women for America, points out that it's one thing for homosexuals to publicly express their appreciation for each other. It's quite another to use the force of law to get the rest of us to accept it. Same-sex marriage is using the force of law to persuade others to accept the unacceptable.

Michelangelo Signorile, a homosexual writer, pointed out further that acceptance of gay marriage could help them redefine marriage in general: "A middle ground might be to fight for same-sex marriage and its benefits and then, once granted, redefine the institution of marriage completely, to demand the right to marry not as a way of adhering to society's moral codes but rather to debunk a myth and radically alter an archaic institution."[3] Thus the destruction of marriage itself is in their sights.

Furthermore, Signorile added that same-sex marriage could give them the legal tool by which they could force their agenda on society: "It is also a chance to wholly transform the definition of family in American culture. It is the final tool with which to dismantle all sodomy statutes, get education about homosexuality and AIDS into public schools, and, in short, usher in a sea change in how society views and treats us."[4] Thus, the push for homosexual marriage is a lot more sweeping than a handful of people expressing their love for each other in a public forum. The long-term consequences could be devastating for society, the family, children, and the church.

If homosexuals really wanted to marry for marriage's sake, then when the opportunity was made available to them, wouldn't it follow that they would quickly rush to walk down the aisle? Yes, but that generally has not happened. It's not about marriage, fidelity, or commitment. It's about forced acceptance. Dr. Timothy J. Dailey of the Family Research Council notes:

> Data from Vermont, Sweden, and the Netherlands reveal that only a small percentage of homosexuals and lesbians identify themselves as being in a committed relationship, with even fewer taking advantage of civil unions or, in the case of the Netherlands, of same-sex "marriage." This indicates that even in the most "gay friendly" localities, the vast majority of homosexuals and lesbians display little inclination for the kind of lifelong, committed relationships that they purport to desire to enter.[5]

Phyllis Schlafly, who played such a leading role in defeating the ERA in another era, notes: "Gays already have the liberty to live their lives as they choose, set up housekeeping, share income and expenses, make contracts and wills, and transfer property. What they are now demanding is respect and social standing for a lifestyle that others believe is immoral (like mixed-gender cohabiting). That amounts to the minority forcing its views on the majority. Nobody is entitled to respect for behavior of which we don't approve."[6]

The leader of the National Gay and Lesbian Task Force says, "Coming out is no longer the sum total of our strategy; we are about power."[7] It's not about lifelong commitment; it's not about fidelity; it's about power.

Inflated Numbers to Force Through Their Agenda

One of the ways proponents of same-sex marriage are able to push their agenda through is by beefing up their numbers. We have heard so often that gays and lesbians comprise 10 percent of the population that we tend to accept it as fact. Where does the number come from? The *Kinsey Report* of fifty years or so ago that stated that 10 percent of the men in America were homosexuals has been shown to be utterly fraudulent. Many of the people surveyed were prisoners or ex-prisoners. There were also prostitutes. The survey was taken in one of the worst sections in Chicago, a red-light kind of area. It would be like someone going out in front of a church on Sunday morning and taking a survey of the people leaving the service as to their religious activities and then making conclusions about the religious attitudes of the whole country. That is, in effect, what Kinsey did, and his report has been exposed as a fraud.

The Guttmacher Report came out recently. Now Guttmacher, the head of Planned Parenthood, was no friend of evangelical Christians by any stretch of the imagination. But his study showed that 1.1 percent of American men were either homosexual or bisexual—a far cry from Kinsey's 10 percent![8]

Another study showed that 2 percent of American men claimed that at one time in their life they had been involved in the homosexual lifestyle but no longer were.[9] Now, friend, did you put those together? Did you get the impact of that, or did you miss it? Let me clarify it. What those two statistics say is that there are far more *ex-homosexuals* in America than there are active homosexuals. So much for the lie that you can't change. More change than don't. Here is an excerpt from a letter from one of them:

> I myself have come out of a homosexual background. However, I have left that part of my life behind to enjoy a fulfilling heterosexual life. It has not been easy, but it has been worthwhile. I now have a loving wife and family and have found a happiness that I did not think was possible in the past. I was deceived for a number of years into believing that there was nothing I could do to change my sexual orientation.
>
> I do not accept the current paradigm that homosexuality is inherited and normal, because I can identify some various obvious environmental influences in my own difficulties.[10]

Here's what the most comprehensive (to date) study on sex in America found regarding self-professed homosexuals, conducted under the auspices of the University of Chicago and released (in the popular version) in a book entitled *Sex in*

America. Here are the numbers they found of self-professed homosexuals and lesbians: "About 1.4 percent of the women said they thought of themselves as homosexual or bisexual and about 2.8 percent of the men identified themselves in this way."[11] That is a far cry from the inflated number of 10 percent.

"Legal" Means "Moral"

The legalization of marriage is so important to homosexuals because in their mind legal means moral. We live in a society where God and His standards have been removed. If you do not go to God's Word for the standards of right or wrong, good or evil, where do you go? To the law. You go to the law for all standards. So if the law says it's legal, then you are OK. You are fine; you are no longer wrong. Even if your own conscience condemns you, it doesn't matter because the law says you are legitimately married, and all is well.

Matt Daniels founded the Alliance for Marriage. This is one of the key groups leading the fight against same-sex marriage. Matt spoke on *The Coral Ridge Hour* with many great insights. He pointed out how the homosexual activists are working on the theory that to many Americans, legal means moral: "That is the reason for the movement to destroy marriage under American law. Those who are behind this movement understand that if they can ever succeed in that effort, they will change the moral and social DNA of America forever, because they will be changing our society at the highest level morally for many people, for many Americans, which is human law, especially when they invoke the Constitution."[12]

We live in scary times—when right is called wrong and evil is called good.

"Monogamy Without Fidelity"

Thus the push for same-sex marriage is the push for the legitimization of homosexuality. So also observes Kerby Anderson, a Christian apologist, radio talk show host, author, speaker, and president of Probe Ministries. He states:

> It is interesting that a number of homosexual activists are talking about this idea of monogamy without fidelity. In other words, they're saying: "Well, we might be married, but we're still going to be promiscuous." . . . [T]his idea of monogamy without fidelity means that when they are talking about marriage, they're not talking about the kind of marriage we're talking about. And a good number of homosexuals, including my uncle and others, don't want to be married. That's not what their goal is. But the argument and the push, I think, for homosexual marriage is, in large part, to try to establish legitimacy. Even the Massachusetts Supreme Judicial Court said, "Separate is rarely equal." In other words, we can't have a separate civil union—we want full marriage rights. Not that most homosexuals that I know want to be married, but they want to have the legal establishment of legitimacy.[13]

Furthermore, Kerby points to the problem of redefining marriage to the point that marriage itself gets redefined—out of existence.

> Part of the issue here has to do with our definition of marriage. We say, right now, that you can be married, anybody can be married, but you have to be married to someone of the opposite sex. They have to be a certain age, they cannot be genetically related to you—there are all sorts of limitations. When you define something, you define what it is, and by doing that you, also, define what it is not. Now, that's not discrimination. You define that two plus two is equal to four, and by defining

that you, also, say that two plus two cannot equal five, six, seven, or eight. So, it is not discrimination in the sense that it's not allowing someone an equal opportunity, it's simply saying that you are defining it in a different way. When we begin to redefine marriage, what we're, ultimately, going to do is undefine marriage. We're going to say that what has traditionally been the very core of Western civilization—and really around the world—is going to be undefined. And when it becomes undefined, it ceases to exist.[14]

It may seem like an exaggeration, but it would seem that our very civilization is at stake. And many Christians don't even realize it.

The Push for Homosexual Adoption

Another reason for the push for same-sex marriage is that it will make it easier for homosexuals and lesbians to legally adopt children. David Gibbs III and his father, David Gibbs, Jr., are involved with the Christian Law Association, which the elder Gibbs founded at their kitchen table in 1969. The Christian Law Association, based in the Tampa, Florida, area, is the longest-lasting and oldest organization fighting for the civil liberties of Christians in the nation.[15] David Gibbs III warns about what same-sex marriage means for homosexuals being able to adopt children.

They want to challenge the right to be able to adopt other people's children in courtrooms across America. When you come into an adoption court, the highest priority is always given to legally married couples. And so, if you can establish that you're a legally married couple, you'll be given a very high priority when you go to adopt other people's children. In many states, homosexuals are not allowed to adopt other people's children, or they're greatly restrained from doing so. And what they're really wanting to do is get this marriage right where they can go into the courts across America and, I believe, their agenda is to adopt all of the unwanted children of America to bring them up with their lifestyle with their way of thinking.[16]

Generally, what is recognized in one state will be recognized in the other states. This is because of the full faith and credit clause of the Constitution.[17] Homosexual activists and liberal legal groups, such as the ACLU, have already threatened to take advantage of this clause. They want homosexual and lesbian couples to get "married" in Massachusetts and then return to their home state and challenge the laws back home.

In our highly litigious age, this could be the beginning of a legal nightmare.

Two Hundred Million Dollars a Year to Redefine Marriage

Matt Daniels points out that those who have taken out long knives to plunge into the heart of traditional marriage are spending a fortune behind the scenes to get this thing passed—through the courts, by unelected judges, where "We the people" have no voice in the matter. They do all of this regardless of the consequences. Says Matt Daniels:

> Most Americans believe it's common sense that marriage is a man and a woman. They believe that gays and lesbians have a right to live as they choose, but they don't have a right to redefine marriage for our entire society. . . . Unfortunately, radical activists who want to destroy the legal road map to marriage and family for selfish reasons, are working through the courts because they want to force the destruction of marriage on the

What's Wrong with Same-Sex Marriage?

American people against the will of the people. And this is a movement that's been in play for about 10 years; about $200 million a year has been spent since 1996 simply on litigation to destroy marriage as a man and a woman. Most people have no idea how big this is. There is a coalition of over a dozen major activist groups that are involved in this effort. They work together systematically—as I said, they spent $200 million, and that was in 1999 alone. They've been spending more every year since, and that's according to their own figures.[18]

One of the active groups pushing for same-sex marriage is the ACLU. In fact, that is the legal group that has brought many of these suits on behalf of same-sex couples in the first place (including the suit in Massachusetts).

The Push for Acceptance in the Schools

Another aspect of the homosexual agenda is the push for acceptance in our schools. Same-sex marriage would make it difficult to stop broad, sweeping promotion of the gay lifestyle in our public schools—divorced from the consequences.

Twenty-six percent of twelve-year-old boys have ambiguities about their sexual identity, which is not unusual. Which one of us men, as twelve-year-old boys, wouldn't have said, "Girls—yuk. Who likes girls?" I never met a girl who was a decent tackle on any football team that I played on as a boy. Of the 26 percent who have sexual confusion, by seventeen that drops to only 5 percent, and by twenty-one, probably down to about 2 percent.

But those younger children are very susceptible to sexual identity teaching. When you teach a little boy from the first grade on that when he grows up, it will be perfectly all right for him to marry Billy, his friend; when you teach first-grade children that Heather has two mommies and Johnny has two daddies, and that's perfectly normal—talk about creating sexual confusion. But that is what is going on in some of our schools. If same-sex marriage becomes fully legalized across the country, then it would be very difficult to stop homosexuals and lesbians from teaching total acceptance of the lifestyle in the schools.

"We are about power," homosexual activists have said. But in their book *After the Ball* Marshall Kirk and Hunter Madsen give the principles of their agenda. Listen to Principle 5:

> Portray gays as victims of circumstance and oppression, not as aggressive challengers.
>
> In any campaign to win over the public, gays must be portrayed as victims in need of protection so that straights will not be inclined to refuse to adopt the role of protector . . . we must forego the temptation to strut our gay pride publicly to such an extent that we will undermine our victim image.[19]

The mask is off. Their real goal, of which same-sex marriage is a major strategy, is revealed—to get straight America to accept their lifestyle.

Homophobia Likened to Racism

If you speak out against homosexuality, even merely saying that it is a sin, from which people can be forgiven and freed, then all of a sudden you're a homophobe and a bigot. Homosexual activists claim that homophobia against them is akin to the racial bigotry directed against blacks for hundreds of years in this country.

Blacks resent this notion. They are born black and can never change. But homosexuals can and sometimes do change.[20]

Matt Daniels points out that many in the Civil Rights movement resent the comparison of the struggle for blacks to get civil rights with the struggle of gays and lesbians for "civil rights." He had this to say about homosexual activists trying to co-opt the Civil Rights movement for themselves:

> The radical activists on the other side are hiding behind the mask of the Civil Rights movement. They are hiding a socially destructive agenda. [They are hiding] behind a mask, which really doesn't belong to them. The Civil Rights movement, of course, was a great movement. It changed America for the better. It was one of the finest hours in the history of this country. And so, social evil always seeks to wear a mask. It seeks to cloak or conceal itself. In this case, you have radical activists who do not represent the African-American community; they don't represent the Latino community; they don't represent the Asian community, and yet they're wrapping themselves in the mantelpiece of the Civil Rights movement in an effort to destroy marriage as the union of male and female in the United States.[21]

Matt has put together an impressive coalition of various groups, from different creeds and colors, all in favor of traditional marriage and opposed to same-sex marriage. One of those is Rev. Walter Fauntroy, who helped organize Dr. Martin Luther King, Jr.'s rally in Washington, DC, ("I have a dream") in 1964. Because Rev. Fauntroy was scheduled to speak out at an Alliance for Marriage press conference, the "tolerant" folks targeted him with a vicious campaign of hate to harass him and his family. Homosexual activists listed his home address, phone number, and e-mail address. And he and his family were besieged by people all over the country. But, says Matt Daniels, this did not deter the minister: "And Walter Fauntroy, to his everlasting credit, spoke anyway. He was not silenced."[22]

One of the points Rev. Fauntroy made at that press conference was that he opposed same-sex marriage because he has seen firsthand what the breakdown of the family does to a community:

> He said he stood next to President Lyndon B. Johnson, along with Martin Luther King Jr., in the West Wing of the White House in 1964 when the Civil Rights Act of 1964 was signed, ending legal segregation in the South. He said the ink on that document was not dry when the blood of young black men started flowing in the streets of our country because of the absence of fathers from the African-American family, because of the breakdown of the family in the inner-city among the African-American community. He said that in 1964 when the Civil Rights Act was signed, 30 percent of African-American kids were born out of wedlock. Today that number is about 80 percent in urban America. And in his comment at the press conference, he said, "If this doesn't stop, we'll be back to slavery when nobody knew their dad. That's why I support the Federal Marriage Amendment."[23]

In short, for homosexual activists to cloak their movement in the guise of civil rights is an exercise in deception.

And yet on May 17, 2004, when gay marriage was made legal in Massachusetts, a number of commentators pointed to the fact that this came fifty years to the day after the Supreme Court decision to give blacks equality in the schools in *Brown vs. the Board of Education.* The commentators said things like, "Back then, the struggle was for justice for black schoolchildren. Now, the struggle is for justice for gays and lesbians." And we could add, "for transgenders, transsexuals, bigamists, polygamists, pedophiles, etc."

Conclusion

So what is the real reason that militant homosexuals are demanding the right to marry? It is to force society to accept their lifestyle as is. Not only to accept it, but to embrace it.

If you think that is an exaggeration, then consider the intolerance you will experience if you dare oppose their agenda, at the hands of those who shout the loudest for tolerance.

3

Intolerance

"Judge not, that you be not judged."

MATTHEW 7:1

Have you ever noticed that those who shout the loudest for tolerance are the most intolerant people in the world if you disagree with them? The militant homosexuals demand tolerance for their lifestyle, but if anyone disagrees, they will experience the full brunt of their intolerance. So the words *tolerance* and *intolerance* take on new and different meanings, depending on who is speaking.

I remember watching a "tolerant" lady on a video one time. A group of militant homosexuals surrounded a church in Madison, Wisconsin, to show their tolerance to the congregation inside. The church members had come to hear a speaker alerting them to the homosexual agenda. So the militants banged garbage can tops and screamed out for tolerance. I have seen the videotape of this protest, and there, plain as day, is one of the protesters yelling at the top of her lungs, "Bring back the lions! Bring back the lions!" The others around her clearly approved of her message: It's time for Christians to again be thrown to the lions.

What's Wrong with Same-Sex Marriage?

In this chapter we will explore how liberals in general and militant homosexuals in particular have distorted the meaning of tolerance and twisted it to mean forced acceptance of their perverted lifestyle. Again, the push for same-sex marriage is simply another step in the push for forced acceptance.

The Redefinition of Tolerance

Those who push for "tolerance" have the view, concerning free speech, that you have complete free speech rights, provided you agree with their views and toe the line. They remind us of the ACLU, which works tirelessly for the free speech rights of those with whom they agree. That's true in 99 percent of the cases, and then, just so they can claim they are nonpartisan and apolitical, they will throw in an occasional defense of a conservative. Meanwhile, woe to you if you dare say, for example, that homosexuality is wrong or say something else so deviant from their opinions.

Sometimes at our church, Coral Ridge Presbyterian Church in Ft. Lauderdale, militant homosexuals surround the building in protest. They have all sorts of tolerant signs with messages like "Stop the Hate!" Jerry Newcombe, coauthor of this book, has made the remark on such occasions, "Oh look, here come the shock troops of tolerance again."

The word *tolerance* has fallen on hard times. It no longer means respect for those with whom you disagree.

Christianity gave birth to tolerance. The good type of tolerance is summarized in Christ's Golden Rule—"So whatever you wish that others would do to you, do also to them, for this is the Law and the Prophets" (Matthew 7:12). This implies respect for others, even if they're different. But today's version of so-called "tolerance" in reality is anything but broad-minded.

Intolerance in the Name of Tolerance

If you don't accept wrong as right, then serious consequences are waiting for you, because homosexual activists not only want your glad acceptance of all of their lifestyles, beliefs, values, and habits as equal with your own—they also want you to participate in what they do. For example:

- At Stanford University, the gay and lesbian alliance promotes a shorts day each spring during which people are exhorted to wear shorts to show their support for homosexual lifestyles. It just so happens that most of the students wear shorts every day; so they are put in a position of either having to change their dress or appear to support what is being done.[1]
- At a Baptist church in San Francisco,[2] homosexual activists not only surrounded the church but pulled at various members trying to get ahold of them to beat them. The church had to lock the doors. The protesters were taking the heavy lawn furniture from in front of the church, and they were trying to break down the doors of the church. They were screaming, "We want your children! We want your children!" Inside, the children were frightened and crying. Fearing the wrath of the homosexual activists, the police did little to stop them.
- At a recent visit to Dartmouth University, a former lesbian speaker, Yvette Schneider, had to receive a police escort to escape out the back door from the wrath of homosexual activists. Her personal effects left at the

podium had to be gathered up and brought to her later. She was brought to the police station for her own safety. As upset as Yvette may have been, the head of the Christian group, which had invited Yvette to speak in the first place, came to the police station "visibly shaken as she sobbed uncontrollably."[3]

There's a whole lot of intolerance going on out there in the name of tolerance.

Similar to the term *tolerance* is the distortion of another word that we are all familiar with—*discrimination*.

Misuse of the Word *Discrimination*

Discrimination simply means to distinguish between several things, especially to distinguish between things that are similar. The word *discriminate* comes from a Latin root, *discernere*. And the root of that word, *cernere*, means to discern. Therefore the word *discern* is the word from which *discriminate* comes; both words mean exactly the same thing.

Some people are twisting this word so that it seems totally bad to discriminate or discern good from evil.

Let's look to the Bible for clarification.

When Solomon first became king of Israel, he prayed to God, asking for an understanding heart so that he might discern between good and bad. Solomon prayed that God would give him an understanding heart and the ability to discriminate between good and evil (2 Chronicles 1:10). If he prayed that prayer today, the ACLU would be all over him if he did so publicly.

The key is the definition of a related term—*acumen*—which means mental clarity and intelligence, to be able to discriminate between several things. In fact, I remember years ago reading that one of the sure signs of a high I.Q. is that a person can discriminate between two similar things, which a person with a lower I.Q. cannot do.

Did you ever hear of a person having a discriminating palate? If you want to be the food critic for a newspaper, you better have one or you are not going to have a job. If you want to be a wine tester, you better have a discriminating palate. If you buy a can of mushroom soup, you will earnestly hope that whoever picked those mushrooms had the ability to discriminate between mushrooms and toadstools.

Racial discrimination has long been understood to be wrong. And it *is* wrong. In Acts 17:26 the Bible declares that by one man, God created *all* the people on the earth. That means that, technically, all of us are related, whether white or black or whatever.

Today few people in this country would try to maintain that racial discrimination is good. We have made much progress since the days when Dr. Martin Luther King, Jr. articulated his dream of a color-blind society. And we have seen gender discrimination outlawed and condemned—even age discrimination. Of course, some discrimination is appropriate. However, some people have smeared the definition of this word so that many Americans naturally assume that all discrimination is bad.

I remember when the city commission of Ft. Lauderdale voted to take away all support from the Boy Scouts of America because they would not allow homosexual Boy Scout leaders to take little boys out into the woods for a nice weekend. Speaking sarcastically, I'm sure all of you would love to have your twelve-year-old spend the weekend with a homosexual Boy Scout leader.

I heard one of the commissioners say, "We just will not allow discrimination of any sort to go on in this city. It is intolerable. We will not tolerate any discrimination about anything." And in the newspaper one of the members of the Broward School Board said, "In our Broward Schools we will have zero tolerance for discrimination of any kind."

Those statements are not true. School boards do discriminate. Will the school board knowingly hire a pedophile? I certainly doubt it. Will they knowingly hire a serial killer? No. Will they knowingly hire one of the leaders of the neo-Nazi party? Not on your life. Would they hire a Ku Klux Klansman to teach social studies in the high school? Never. We must discriminate against all of those people.

Unfortunately, often the only people some activists want to discriminate against—and therefore rule out—are Christians. Some people will tolerate anything but those who have beliefs in dogma and absolutism. Who are they? The United Nations in its Declaration on Tolerance tolerates anything except Christianity because our faith is an absolute religion. God is the ultimate absolute. His Word is absolute truth. His Son is the absolute divine Savior. So who is the United Nations turning their guns on when they say that they will not allow dogmatism or absolutism? Dear friends, if you don't know it, those guns are pointed right at you.

The difference between heterosexuality and homosexuality is often couched in terms of differences in tastes. You like chocolate; I like vanilla. Some prefer the straight lifestyle, others the gay lifestyle. Others choose something in between. This lack of discernment ignores the causes and consequences of these choices.

Barbarism vs. Civilization

I believe that discrimination is the difference between barbarism and civilization. When the ability to choose between good and evil is lost or pounded into the mud, a society will eventually degenerate into the barbarism of the jungle. And that's what's going on in our country today. But notice that I am talking about discriminating between the bad and the good, not between black and white, old and young, male and female. We are talking about *moral discrimination*.

What if a school administrator says, "It is the mission of public schools not to tolerate intolerance"? That's their purpose? Our students have lower math skills and science knowledge than children from virtually every other industrialized nation, but our children are learning to tolerate evil.

The educational elites will tolerate students shooting other students in the classroom. They will tolerate an epidemic of drugs. They will tolerate alcoholism. They will tolerate promiscuous sex. They will tolerate illegitimate children being born to children. They will tolerate blasphemy of every sort. But they won't tolerate anybody who will not accept all the beliefs and values of everyone else.

Tolerance may indeed be the dominant theme of the modern curriculum of our public schools. The authors of a recent study of American high schools concluded, "Tolerating diversity is the moral glue that holds schools together."[4] Another study of American history textbooks found toleration presented as "the only 'religious' idea worth remembering."

That's all that's left—just the smile on the face of the Cheshire cat. Tolerance is the idea, said one of the writers in the book *Teaching Tolerance*, that is universally relevant to virtually every class. It belongs everywhere in the curriculum, and teachers are being told how to teach it in every single subject. From history to literature to mathematics, the children are learning tolerance—the last virtue of an immoral society.

Kenneth S. Stern writes, "Teaching diversity should be an educational mission that saturates the campus."[5]

Yet for four thousand years a virtuous citizen was thought of as a person who believed in God, a person who believed in morality, who lived a life of virtue and did his best to maintain morality in the society—and rejected immorality and ungodliness.

But no longer. Today's "virtuous citizen" may be a criminal. A drug addict. An alcoholic. A thief. A pervert. A child molester. He may be any of these things, but as long as he is tolerant and objects to intolerance, he is all right.

Postmodernism

You may remember that modernism (sometimes called rationalism or identified as the Age of Reason) is supposed to have begun at the fall of the Bastille in 1789, the beginning of the French Revolution. No longer were we living in the Age of Faith, but now the Age of Reason and modernism had been ushered in. The Age of Reason reached its pinnacle in the atheistic, scientific evolutionary, socialistic USSR—the Soviet Union. And that age ended with the collapse of the Berlin Wall in 1989, two hundred years after the French Revolution. We have passed through the Age of Modernity, and we are now in the Postmodern Age.

A total concept of "feeling" is involved in Postmodernism.

No Feelings Hurt

The postmodernist says, "Reason has failed. We must resort to feeling." How often do you hear people say, "Well, I feel that _____." "I feel that Washington, DC, is the capital of this country." No, I don't feel that. I think and know it. But it's always "I feel." We have even invented a new civil right: the right for my feelings to be protected.

Recently a young lady in one of the high schools sued the school because they sang a song there that had some religious words in it—one of our patriotic songs. She said these words hurt her feelings. The whole school ground to a halt, and the courts moved into action. "We cannot have anybody's feelings hurt," they said.

The universal individual is part of Postmodernism. We no longer have countries. We no longer have the human race. Just individuals and their feelings, and they must not be offended. And so the courts threw this song—and others like it—out because this girl's feelings were hurt. We have gone from a democracy—the government of the people, by the people, and for the people—to a government of the sovereign individual— or should I say more accurately, of the sovereign individual's feelings.

Speak the Truth in Love

We must realize how the other side has hijacked the meanings of good words like *tolerance* and *discrimination*. We can experience a true change in this country if we get back to an understanding of what God sees as right and wrong and stick with His definitions.

Jesus told us that we would be known by our love, which is the mark of the true disciple of Christ, and love includes discernment and concern for our neighbors or friends if they happen to be on the wrong path. Love includes telling people that they need to repent.

Contrast with How the Media Treat Christians and Homosexuals

As with just about any problem in America, half the problem is the media. They are anti-Christian for the most part. They are certainly left of center, and if anyone doubts it, just read the daily reports of the Media Research Center of Alexandria, Virginia. They document the daily leftward tilt of the mainstream media. Two excellent books on the subject are by Bernard Goldberg, former twenty-eight-year veteran of CBS News. His best-selling books, *Bias* (Regnery, 2001) and *Arrogance* (Warner Books, 2003), provide ample proof of the media's leftward tilt.

How does the media feel about homosexuality? The answer is obvious because it confronts us virtually each night on the evening news. A study of the media elite, the top decision-makers of the news media, found that 80 percent "do not regard homosexual relations as wrong" and that 86 percent "support the rights of homosexuals to teach in public schools."[6]

So how does that impact what we see?

In September 1998, when two rednecks killed homosexual Matthew Shepherd in Wyoming, the media never stopped commenting on it. It was instantly defined as a hate crime. A year later, in September 1999, a man shouting anti-Christian expletives barged into Wedgewood Baptist Church in Ft. Worth during a service filled with young people. He shot and killed seven. The media and Attorney General Janet Reno never got around to calling this a hate crime. They spoke as if the motives were unclear and went to the grave with the troubled shooter who shot himself too. Few Americans have forgotten about Matthew Shepherd because it was so widely reported. Few have remembered the incident at Wedgewood because it was so underreported (comparatively).[7]

The overall impression you get from many in our culture is that religion is a repressive force. In a recent HBO special Ellen DeGeneres played a lesbian, and she and her lover, played by Sharon Stone, were trying to have a baby. As Norm MacDonald once quipped, their plan had a hitch though—they were both women. So they decided to go to the sperm bank to choose a kid. As they reviewed the different potential options, the one thing they didn't want was a "religious tighta—."

And so it goes.

It's well-known that you can hold up Christians, either evangelicals, fundamentalists, or Catholics, to ridicule, but virtually no other subgroup. In fact, I've now come to hold the opinion that liberals who oppose prejudice, racism, and bigotry of any kind actually believe that it is bigoted to *not* treat conservative Christians with bigotry. In other words, their understanding of tolerance demands that they be intolerant of Christians—otherwise, they're being intolerant. In short, they abhor bigotry of any kind, except when directed at conservative Christians, who deserve to be discriminated against, they say.

We once corresponded with syndicated columnist Cal Thomas about Christian-bashing in general, and he made an interesting remark. He actually welcomes this ridicule, provided it isn't something we bring on ourselves: "To a very large extent, I welcome 'Christian bashing' if it is for righteousness' sake. I think we should look for ways to live even more righteously that the 'bashing' might increase. After all, if they hated Him, they're supposed to hate us too, right?"[8]

The homosexual activist says in effect, "You must show me

tolerance and accept my lifestyle as is. If you don't, you will feel the full brunt of my intolerance."

Conclusion

And so we find ourselves in a culture where those who call evil good and good evil are tolerated—they have their own talk shows and are the darlings of the media. On the other hand, those who stand for what God says about morality—including opposition to same-sex marriage—are the targets of the intolerance of those who clamor the most for tolerance.

4

The Top Twelve Reasons We're Opposed to Same-Sex Marriage

And since they did not see fit to acknowledge God,
God gave them up to a debased mind to do
what ought not to be done.

ROMANS 1:28

I n this chapter we want to explore some of the leading reasons to oppose same-sex marriage. We will hear from many thoughtful Christian leaders as to why they are opposed to it.

Reason #1: God opposes homosexuality.

This reason alone is sufficient for us.

In the next chapter we will explore a multitude of the Scriptures condemning homosexuality. Putting homosexuality in the larger context, the Bible condemns all sexual relationships outside of marriage. God's idea is one man and one woman for life, as stated in Genesis 2:24:

Therefore a man shall leave his father and his mother and hold
fast to his wife, and they shall become one flesh.

This gets back to the very creation itself. God created woman for and from the man and led her to Adam. Here is the standard for all time; and as followers of God, we cannot accept anything else. God's love and blessing are on those who live His way, and we cannot be quiet anymore when people want to legalize their immorality.

Today people sometimes say that Jesus never condemned homosexuality. This only shows their ignorance. When He condemned *porneia*, He certainly condemned homosexuality. And in Matthew 15:19 and Mark 7:21 Jesus did indeed condemn *porneia*, from which our modern word *pornography* is derived. This word is translated as "sexual immorality" in some of our English translations, but it really stands for a multitude of sexual sins, all condemned in the Old Testament Law: premarital sex, adultery, homosexuality, incest, bestiality. Furthermore, Jesus put His seal of approval on the Old Testament as God's Word (Matt. 5:17-19), and, again, the Old Testament condemns homosexuality as well. To say Jesus approved of homosexuality is an argument by silence, and it falls short of the facts.

Reason #2: Same-sex marriage (and same-sex conjugal relations) goes against the natural order.

Male with male and female with female just does not work physically. It does not fit. It goes against nature, and it creates all kind of problems. As one wag put it, "God made Adam and Eve—He didn't make Adam and Steve."

Pastor Bob Coy of Calvary Chapel in Ft. Lauderdale gives a simple analogy. If you have a light bulb out and you call the maintenance man to fix it, he doesn't bring over a new fixture—as if to somehow attach one fixture to another. Nor do we try and attach one light bulb to another. Instead, they attach a bulb (sometimes called male) to the fixture (sometimes called female).

Similarly, we don't try and take an electric plug (sometimes called a male) and try and attach it into another plug (another male). They don't fit. Instead, the plug fits into an outlet (sometimes called a female).

In short, homosexuality is against nature. The plumbing doesn't work. We weren't designed this way.

When homosexuals ignore nature, first, they invite into their own bodies all sorts of infectious diseases. Chapter 6 explores how deadly this lifestyle can be.

Second, there are emotional problems. Even in every homosexual relationship, there is a male and a female role. One of them plays the male or the dominant partner, and the other plays the female. This shows you that by nature God has made us male and female. He has made each sex to complement the other.

A dark secret—downplayed by our media—is the domestic abuse that sometimes characterizes the homosexual lifestyle. When a gay lover cheats on his "beloved," there can be hell to pay. Like the man who beat his male lover senseless with a desktop telephone because the latter had threatened to walk out on the former. As Leslie Unruh of the Abstinence Clearinghouse once pointed out, there's no condom strong enough to prevent a broken heart.

Matt Daniels of the Alliance for Marriage adds the point that same-sex households discriminate against the missing parent. Homosexual couples discriminate against mom. Lesbian couples discriminate against dad:

> If you say that two men living together can provide the same healthy environment as a mom and a dad, you are making a profoundly negative statement about women. You are saying that women, half of the human race, are irrelevant to the raising of children, that they make no unique contribution to the

raising of the next generation. It is a profoundly derogatory statement about women. Flip it over on its head: You talk about two lesbians raising a child. You're making a profoundly negative statement about men, half the human race, dads, fathers; you're saying they're unnecessary, irrelevant, children don't need them. Well, we know from the data that both of those statements are flat-out wrong, that kids need a mom and a dad. The data's on our side. And it's really those who are trying to destroy the family who should be apologizing for their selfish, self-interested efforts, to radically destroy an institution which has unique benefits for kids . . . the underlying thrust of the effort to destroy marriage is profoundly anti-child.[1]

Reason #3: It goes against all of recorded history.

We are looking at about five thousand years of recorded history with marriage being one man and one woman together for their mutual enjoyment and the protection of their children. Yes, there was homosexuality in antiquity, and there has been polygamy in several places in the world, and it is still practiced among Muslims and tribal people (and some Mormons). But the norm has been marriage between two people of the opposite sex. Homosexuality has in virtually all societies been viewed as a perversion and not normal. For example, Dr. Joseph Nicolosi—a psychologist who has had success in helping homosexuals leave that lifestyle—writes in his book *Reparative Therapy of Male Homosexuality*, "A classic study of 76 cultures revealed that no culture views homosexuality to be equal to, or of higher status than, heterosexuality. Further, even in those cultures in which homosexuality is tolerated, exclusive homosexuality is never sanctioned."[2]

Should we throw overboard an institution that has served our world well for thousands of years, just so we don't offend a small but vociferous group? We think not. Marriage is the bedrock of any civilized society. Same-sex marriage contradicts a recorded tradition that goes back through all of recorded history and virtually all cultures.

Less than two decades ago the United States Supreme Court recognized the long-standing tradition against men sleeping with men and women with women. Listen to what former Chief Justice Warren Burger wrote in *Bowers v. Hardwick* in 1986, which upheld a sodomy statute: "To hold that the act of homosexual sodomy is somehow protected as a fundamental right would be to cast aside millennia of moral teaching."[3] Amen. Tragically, seventeen years later the Supreme Court revisited the issue and cast aside five thousand years of morality. The Constitution hasn't changed—only those who interpret it.

Reason #4: It will hurt children.

When Rosie O'Donnell's six-year-old son asked, "Mommy, why can't I have a daddy?" he was pleading not just for what he wanted, but for what he needed as well. Rosie's answer, "Because I'm the kind of mommy who wants another mommy," illustrates the adult selfishness that drives the same-sex marriage movement.

Three decades into America's epidemic of fatherlessness, we know that depriving children of fathers damages them and their future. Same-sex marriage will rob children of what they need most: the love and nurture of both a mother and a father.

How come American life has deteriorated for so many millions of us, especially our children? How come some of our inner cities have become like war zones? Because of the breakdown of the family. As Matt Daniels says, "The decline of marriage is a disaster for kids and for society."[4] Same-sex marriage as a norm will drive another nail in the coffin of the American family, and children will be the biggest victims of all.

According to Chuck Colson, there are already 2.1 million people in prison in America. A lot of this reflects the breakdown of the family.[5] We do not need to add to the problem. Children need to be nurtured and protected. They need time and effort and constant care. When a woman is pregnant, she is looking at twenty years of care and unselfish sacrifice ahead of her. Gay marriages are not stable. If such persons want to adopt another person's child, how can they give that child the next twenty years—especially when they are participating in behaviors that will likely (statistically) cause many of them to die long before the time the child reaches adulthood? Why should these children be deprived of everything from grandparents to cousins? Homosexual relationships are also more violent than heterosexual marriages; so their homes are not safe places for children to be.

And since the adults are already involved in perversion, how safe are those children from sexual abuse? Anthony Falzarano, former head of PFOX (Parents and Friends of Ex-gays), said that approximately 75 percent of homosexuals and lesbians were sexually molested as children.[6] We know that early sexual abuse leads to all manner of emotional and physical trauma. To protect children from being adopted by gays is one of the foremost reasons for stopping homosexual marriages.

The scandal of molestation by some priests in the Roman Catholic Church is well-publicized. What is not well-known is that for the most part it is a *homosexual* problem. Very few of the victims are little girls. They are almost always young men— mostly boys who are post-puberty. In short, it's more of a gay scandal than a pedophile scandal, but this is not made clear because of our biased media.

As an attorney, Craig Parshall has had to defend Christian parents who have had a spouse leave and join the homosexual lifestyle. Custody battles over those children can get very ugly. He notes, "If you get a case in the wrong hands of the wrong judge with the wrong political or legal agenda, you will have these children the victims of gay mentality, whether we like it or not."[7]

If gay marriage is equal under the law to a traditional heterosexual marriage, are we not saying that one family structure is equal to the other, or no better than the other, when it comes to raising children? But study after study shows that children do better in a two-parent family (clarification: one mom and one dad). Gay marriage is not good and just for society. To please one small group of homosexuals, shall we sacrifice the good of all the children who will be deprived of a mom and a dad?

Reason #5: It cheapens marriage.

As counterfeit money lowers the value of real money, such counterfeit marriage could destroy the real thing. If anybody can get married to anyone, it's not special anymore; and it's definitely not sacred.

Genevieve Wood of the Family Research Council points out:

When you dilute something, you take away what's special about it. When you come in and you counterfeit something, you cheapen it. And the reality is the reason we don't allow people to counterfeit money is because it cheapens the real thing. That's what happens when you counterfeit marriage. When you say that marriage is no longer just a man and a woman, it can be any other of a variety of arrangements, all of a sudden, it's not very special anymore and, all of a sudden, we're suggesting that one family structure is no better than another for raising the next generation. And in a politically correct world, that may be the thing to say. But the truth is we know better. There are some family structures that do better at raising children than others and, unfortunately, it's children who are victims when we suggest otherwise.[8]

There is empirical data to back up the point that same-sex marriage dilutes the real thing. It can be found, for one place, in Scandinavia. Stanley Kurtz, a research fellow at the Hoover Institution, says that marriage in Scandinavia is dying, partly because of the "marriage-like same-sex registered partnerships" in place now for more than ten years. Writes Kurtz:

> Data from European demographers and statistical bureaus show that a majority of children in Sweden and Norway are now born out of wedlock, as are 60 percent of first-born children in Denmark. In socially liberal districts of Norway, where the idea of same-sex registered partnerships is widely accepted, marriage itself has almost entirely disappeared.[9]

An irony of this is that the coauthor of this book, Jerry Newcombe, and his wife, Kirsti, were married in Norway in her home church (1980). The worst area of Norway, marriage-wise, says Kurtz—where marriage is really dying—is the Nordland region. Jerry's wife points out that Nordland is the most heathen portion of that country. Among the Christians of Norway—and there are many, thankfully—Nordland, which is above the Arctic circle, is often referred to as being above "the moral circle." It is an area of Norway where Christianity has never fully penetrated and where it has had the least influence.

Reason #6: Same-sex marriage will unleash a legal nightmare.

First on the agenda of many of those gays who got "married" in Massachusetts recently is to go back to their own states to challenge the laws there. Even the states that have passed the DOMA (Defense of Marriage Act) are far from safe. Those laws will be challenged.

Attorney Craig Parshall notes that the Massachusetts Supreme Court has created a constitutional nightmare:

> What they were saying is that it's not only required legally, but it's a moral mandate for us to accept homosexuality as a chosen behavior. Now, the reason that's shocking is because Massachusetts, if they continue their recognition of homosexual marriage, will then create, really, a Constitutional crisis for every other state in the union.[10]

That's because of the full faith and credit clause of the Constitution, by which something in one state—in this case, marriage—is routinely recognized as legal in another state. And Parshall adds that this "will create a crisis that will have to be weeded out, eventually, by our U.S. Supreme Court. And until that time, there will be chaos in terms of definition of family in every city, every county, every state in this union."[11]

We already have enough lawsuits in America and enough legal nightmares. This will only add fuel to the fire.

The next mess is marriage benefits, including everything from Social Security, wills, joint IRS forms, and bank accounts. The health benefits will be a nightmare too. We will all have to pay raised premiums to cover the rising costs. The costs of an irresponsible, unhealthy lifestyle are high.

If a gay marriage is of equal value under the law, then there can be no discernment and no preference shown to traditional marriage. What will that mean for the public schools from kindergarten to state colleges? Johnny will have to learn about adult perversion from kindergarten up. The schools will be a main recruiting ground for homosexuality. The legal implications to the military and all the federal institutions too are staggering.

Again here are insights from author and attorney Craig Parshall:

> When you look at the problem of divorce, it's the problem of instability of a relationship with a child being a pawn in that relationship. The average homosexual relationship lasts a few years, at most. The average homosexual relationship is one that incurs numerous other sex partners and this is, statistically, beyond debate. If we take that milieu and we put the legal imprimatur of local or state or federal governmental approval, we are asking for the worst ever opportunity case, divorce case, and same-sex marriage all rolled into one. And our court system will, then, be faced with weeding out these problems, when divorces between same-sex couples start burgeoning. And you know that's going to happen, because these are, basically, unstable units to begin with.[12]

The fascinating thing about this is that Bob Knight, then of the Family Research Council, now of the Culture and Family Institute, was warning about all these things in the mid-1990s. He said the following in 1997:

> The implications [of same-sex marriage] are endless. Federal welfare benefits, state welfare benefits. We are a society that has so many interlocking webs of influence from state laws and federal laws to local laws, corporate policies, academic policies, you name it. All of this can be subverted if you subvert the moral law itself at the most fundamental level.[13]

Reason #7: It will sink the culture from civilization to barbarism—a major step.

Craig Parshall points out, "There's never been a society—ever in the history of the world—that has ever survived this kind of perversion."[14] And he adds that the United States is not exempt.[15]

The approval of immorality is a major step for any declining society on its way from civilization to barbarianism. The family has been the building block of civilization for millennia. Anytime a society has tried to abolish it, the result has been a disaster—from ancient Rome to the Soviet Union to the kibbutzes of Israel and the hippy communes of the 1960s. When the family unravels, society unravels. The traditional family cannot coexist with same-sex marriage for any length of time.

When the Viking society of Norway went from barbarian to civilized (because of Christianity), polygamy was outlawed in A.D. 1029. Today in Norway most young couples do not bother to get married. Some marry after a child or two, but parenting has been separated from marriage, and there seems to be little reason for marriage. How did Norway and other Scandinavian countries reach this nadir in family life? Again, by legalizing same-sex unions about a decade ago—granting homosexuals (and cohabiting couples) the same exact rights as marriage. By cheapening marriage, the Scandinavian countries have cheapened the family. And as the family goes, so goes society.

Reason #8: It destabilizes all of society.

Society cannot remain stable when there is no permanency. The greatest sense of belonging has been provided by the traditional family. We know who we are because we belong to a family unit with all persons sharing the same last name. Who are responsible for the children? And who will care for the elderly? Already we see the practice of warehousing the elderly—often hiding them away in institutions that smell bad. The instability that will overtake us if same-sex marriage is not stopped will affect all areas of society, from schools to jobs to retirement.

Matt Daniels has created a powerful analogy. Marriage is like a road map that society can use to get back on track:

> Our laws still have enshrined in them the road map to marriage: marriage is a man and a woman. This is a road map that sends a positive message to kids about marriage, family and their future. The problem is if you're lost in the woods, but you have a road map, you have a fighting chance of getting back on the trail. If you have no road map at all, you're really lost. And we know from statistics that God builds into the human heart the desire to live according to His plan. The polls show that young people in this country have a deep desire for lifelong marriage. They're pessimistic about whether they'll ever achieve it, but it's something that they want because God put that in their heart. If we can give them the road map, they have a chance of doing better than the generation of the '60s, the generation of the '70s and the '80s; they have a fighting chance of finding their way back on the trail.[16]

Massachusetts governor Mitt Romney wrote a guest editorial in the *Wall Street Journal*, in which he affirmed that marriage (one man, one woman) is "the basic building block of society." He noted, "That benefits are given to married couples and not to singles or gay couples has nothing to do with discrimination; it has everything to do with building a stable new generation and nation."[17]

Reason #9: It opens Pandora's box in the legalization of all sexual perversions. What's next?

When one form of immorality is legalized, it opens the door for others as well. How far behind is NAMBLA—the North American Man/Boy Love Association? Already there is a push to lower the age of consent. We are opening the floodgates to all kinds of perversions. What if someone wants to "marry" his dog to get medical benefits? Is that OK too? Where do you draw the line?

Same-sex marriage leads us down a slippery slope. To say that marriage is no longer between one man and one woman opens the door for marriage to mean anything. Some of the proponents for same-sex marriage have already stated outright that their goal is to destroy marriage altogether.

Liberal commentator and former co-host of *Crossfire* Michael Kinsley wrote a guest editorial in the *Washington Post* in the summer of 2003. Listen to these chilling words from an article entitled "Abolish Marriage: Let's Really Get the Government Out of Our Bedrooms": "[The] solution is to end the institution of marriage, or rather, the solution is to end the monopoly on marriage. And yes, if three people want to get married, or one person wants to marry herself and someone else wants to conduct a ceremony and declare them married, let 'em. If you and your government aren't implicated, what do you care? If marriage were an entirely private affair, all the disputes over gay marriages would become irrelevant."[18] Thus says Kinsley and others. They want marriage itself redefined out of existence.

And if same-sex marriage is all right, then with what moral authority can we condemn polygamy?

Reason #10: It will hurt women for many reasons, including polygamy.

There is already a suit in Utah by which a polygamist is trying to legally marry his wives (plural). This is bad for everyone—including the children and the women. We forget that women could be among the hardest hit victims.

What's Wrong with Same-Sex Marriage?

Attorney Craig Parshall has great insights on this issue:

> When you look at protection of marriage to one man and one woman, the argument, of course, could be made that once you violate that basic institution and say: all comers can be entitled to a marriage license, first you start with multiple wives or multiple husbands. And polygamy is a problem for the stability of any society, because it's never been proven to be a stable unit. In fact, you look to the Old Testament, and some of the biggest problems that Solomon had was because of his inter-marrying with multiple wives. And I think God's lesson to history is, when He designed marriage in the Garden, He didn't pick multiple mates, He picked one man and one woman as the perfect paradigm of what marriage is supposed to look like. That wasn't by accident. That was by Divine Design.[19]

Polygamy is totally unacceptable to most women. The sharing of a husband is the end of real marriage and partnership. It's the end of female dignity. It leads to jealousy, anxiety, and stress. If we now allow homosexuals to marry without stopping this, we will have unleashed a destructive force that will have as its first victims women and children.

Reason #11: Same-sex marriages can produce no natural offspring.

This argument is a variation of Reason #2, that homosexuality is against nature. In biblical times it was a curse to be barren. Now in our culture some homosexuals derisively call heterosexual parents "breeders." Contrary to the mood of our culture, children are a blessing of the Lord—not a curse.

There are no natural offspring in a same-sex marriage. Therefore, in one sense it is a barren relationship. Modern science seems to be changing that scenario, but it is still against nature. In fact, we have already seen some horrific legal battles as lesbian ex-lovers battle for custody of a child born by one of them who had been artificially inseminated.

Homosexuality is destructive to society because there can be no natural offspring. The West is currently on a self-destructive course. From birth control to abortion, we are not multiplying. When you add the growing homosexual population, we are decreasing. In contrast to the Western one to two children per household, the Muslims are having about ten to twelve, and they keep growing. They have a clear idea of their goal of world domination, and they are winning in the bedroom.

We don't want to be alarmists here, but we must not forget that the Muslims are waiting in the wings. It is the goal now—and ever has been—for Islam to take over the whole world. If the Western world stumbles and falls and can't get up, heaven help us. History shows us that anarchy always leads to tyranny. The French Revolution leaps to mind. Fanatical Muslims salivate at the prospect of the United States falling irreparably. The acceptance of same-sex marriage could hasten that end. May it never be!

Reason 12: *The situation is scary for Christians because we become the bad guys. Same-sex marriage will criminalize Christianity.*

One goal of the homosexual activists is to silence the churches. Hate crime laws and anti-discrimination laws will mean the criminalization of anyone who dares to disagree with their perversions. All who will not call the practice normal will find themselves being labeled homophobic or worse. Same-sex marriage proponents have confused value with standard. We are not allowed to have any standards anymore, in order to deem homosexuals valuable human beings with the same rights as everybody else. As a matter of fact, they have equal rights under the law as citizens. But we believe they should not have special rights.

Matt Daniels of the Alliance for Marriage points out this tendency for Christians to be targeted:

> We will also see our children persecuted in the schools. We've already had a foretaste of this in many states. If marriage as a man and a woman is destroyed under American law, children in every public school in the United States and also increasingly in private schools will be taught that their own parents are on a par with bigots and racists for telling them that marriage is a man and a woman. The folks behind this revolution are absolutely determined to force that on our children. And the only way to stop them is to fight the battle to save marriage.[20]

Bob Knight points out:

> I don't think we're very far away from a time when churches will lose their tax exempt status if they don't perform homosexual weddings for instance. I think they'll lose their tax exempt status if a pastor speaks out from the pulpit against homosexuality because the government will say, "Look, we have an overriding interest in eliminating discrimination that trumps your religious freedom." They've done that in many cases already. Take Georgetown University for instance. At Georgetown University, a Catholic school in Washington, D.C., a group of homosexual students wanted to form a club and get formal recognition. The school administration said you can't do that. Catholic teaching is that homosexuality is a sin. The homosexuals took their case to court, and they won in court. . . . There have been other cases where the religious exemption is overridden by a compelling government interest, and that's what this whole sweep of homosexual civil rights is all about. It's to trump religion's protections

and place biblically oriented people in a vulnerable position where they can be prosecuted for not promoting homosexuality.[21]

These things are not just theory. Just look to our northern neighbor, Canada, which has passed some scary bills that take away the free speech rights of Christians to speak out against homosexuality. For example, officials in London, Ontario, fined a Christian mayor $10,000 because he refused to proclaim "Gay Pride Day."[22] Also *World* magazine notes: "A Christian businessman in Toronto was fined $5,000 for refusing to print materials for a gay-rights group."[23] We are in for some dark days if we do not take a stand now.

Harvard Law professor Mary Ann Glendon points out the irony of all this:

> Gay-marriage proponents use the language of openness, toler-ance and diversity, yet one foreseeable effect of their success will be to usher in an era of intolerance and discrimination the likes of which we have rarely seen before. Every person and every religion that disagrees will be labeled as bigoted and openly discriminated against. The ax will fall most heavily on religious persons and groups that don't go along.[24]

Conclusion

Because of all of these reasons and more, we are opposed to same-sex marriage. Because of the seriousness of this and what it could mean for our society, we believe a Federal Marriage Amendment would be the best way to fight this potential tyranny. For more information, please see the Epilogue.

Thus far we have explored the importance of marriage and how same-sex marriage is a cheap counterfeit that will destroy the real thing if it gets fully accepted. Now we move on to Part II, where we will look at what the Bible, social science, and experience itself says about homosexuality. What causes it, what is the lifestyle like (without going into too many details), and can they change? We believe the answer is yes, if they want to, through the power of Jesus Christ.

Homosexuality:
Its Cause, Effects,
and Cure

5

Entertaining Angels Unawares

And they called to Lot,
"Where are the men who came to you tonight?
Bring them out to us, that we may know them."
GENESIS 19:5

An ancient story—a modern problem. In fact, it is one of the greatest moral, spiritual, and social problems of the last several decades. I refer to the problem of sodomy and to the story in Genesis 19, wherein the city of Sodom gave its name to live in infamy in the perversion of sodomy—or as it is called today, homosexuality or "the gay lifestyle," if you prefer. It certainly is something that has grabbed a lot of attention. The legalization of gay marriages in Massachusetts and the attempt to force it on the rest of the country is another effort to shove this issue in our faces.

I trust that the details of Genesis 19 are fairly clear to you. You recall that God said that the wickedness of Sodom had come up to heaven, and He was going to destroy the city. Henry F. Halley in his *Halley's Bible Handbook* makes a fascinating observation about this: "These cesspools of iniquity [Sodom and Gomorrah] were only a few miles from Hebron, the home of Abraham, and from Jerusalem, the home of Melchizedek; yet so vile, their stench reached heaven."[1]

Abraham pled that the Lord would not destroy the righteous with the wicked, and if there were fifty righteous within the city, God agreed He would not destroy it. He then agreed He would spare the city if forty could be found . . . if thirty could be found there . . . if twenty could be found there . . . nor would He destroy the city for ten's sake (Gen. 18:23-32). Apparently there were not so many as ten righteous people in the city of Sodom. So the city was destroyed.

Remember that the two other angels, appearing merely as men (the other was actually the Lord Jehovah in a theophany—a brief appearance in human form), came into Sodom at evening. Lot, who was sitting at the gate, had years earlier chosen the fertile plains that surrounded Sodom. It was called the Garden of God, a place of great abundance and leisure and wealth. Lot invited these gentlemen to come into his home to wash their feet, rest, eat, and rise early the next morning. They said, "No; we will spend the night in the town square" (Gen. 19:2).

That caused Lot a great deal of concern. He urged them to sleep in his house because he no doubt had seen what had happened to others in that infamous city who endeavored to spend the night in the square or in the street.

So they turned in. He fixed a meal for them, and they did eat. But before they could even lie down to sleep, the men of Sodom surrounded the house. "And they called to Lot, 'Where are the men who came to you tonight? Bring them out to us, that we may know them'" (Gen. 19:5).

Scripture Twisting

It is interesting that homosexuality and the homosexuals who have literally created a revolution in our society and culture have moved into the churches. In fact, they have established a whole denomination of Metropolitan Community Churches; there are some two hundred such churches across the country.

It's disheartening to witness the rising of this so called "Christian" gay movement. It isn't enough for them to choose their unnatural lifestyle; they want to retain the blessings of the church. So they fool themselves into thinking that God somehow accepts them just as they are—in their unrepentant sin. Some of those who speak out for special rights for homosexuals claim to be Christians, and they claim that homophobia against them is akin to the racial bigotry directed against blacks for hundreds of years in this country.

They have been engaged in trying to twist the Scriptures to justify their sin. This reminds me of Peter who talks in one of his epistles about those who "twist" the Scriptures "to their own destruction" (2 Pet. 3:16). That is exactly what these people are doing. They have redefined the sin of sodomy and the sin of the sodomite as being simply inhospitality.

There is no doubt the people of Sodom were inhospitable. They were sinners like other people in that they were proud. They were wealthy. They were, unfortunately, idle much of the time, and they lusted after the pleasures of this life. They did not care for the poor, we are told (Ezek. 16:49-50). But the men of Sodom also committed an abomination before the Lord, and it was this sin, this abomination, that caused them to be destroyed.

The homosexual churches support their view by claiming

that when the men of Sodom said, "Bring them out to us, that we may know them," they simply wanted to get acquainted. It is true that the word *yada* in Hebrew, which means "to know," is used exactly like it is used in English—in two different ways. It may mean simply intellectual knowledge, getting acquainted with something or someone, learning about something or someone, just as we use the word. Or it might mean that intimate knowledge that comes from sexual intercourse. So we read that "Cain *knew* his wife, and she conceived" (Gen. 4:17); and So-and-so *knew* his wife, and she conceived and bore a child. *Know* is used in both senses, just as we use the word. In fact, in jurisprudence in America today there is something called "carnal knowledge," and that is the same kind of use of the word.

But homosexual activists say that is not what the word means here—it simply means they wanted to get acquainted with the people, to get to know them. But what did Lot say? He *knew* these men of the city, and how did he respond? "And [Lot] said, 'I beg you, my brothers, do not act so wickedly'" (Gen. 19:7). If they just wanted to get to know them, what was wicked about that? Can you imagine me saying, "Now I know that some of you are planning to go over to a popular restaurant after church this Sunday and get acquainted with some strangers. Do not act so wickedly." That is absurd.

And so all of the homosexuals' logic and their twisting and wresting of Scriptures is absurd. But they deceive the gullible, those for whom the wish is the father of the thought, those who easily fall prey to that.

Not only did Lot know what they were going to do, but the men of Sodom themselves knew what they were going to do. Listen to what they said: "This fellow came to sojourn, and he has become the judge. Now we will deal worse with you than with them" (v. 9). That doesn't sound like they just wanted to get acquainted.

You would think they would have responded to Lot by saying, "Why, Lot, old friend, all we want to do is get acquainted with your guests and show them some hospitality." Inhospitable? My friends, if they simply wanted to get acquainted and be hospitable, then that means that "the men of the city, the men of Sodom, both young and old, all the people to the last man, surrounded the house" that they might "know" the visitors. If that word *yada* merely means hospitality, then that was the most hospitable town I have ever heard of in my life! They get the gold medal for hospitality. Have you ever been to a city where people turned out from every quarter, where all the men just wanted to get to know you? I never have.

To say that their sin was inhospitality is utterly absurd. It reminds me that the weakness of any argument depends upon the absurd lengths to which some people will go to try to defend it. These people will go to any extent and length to try to defend their perversion as actually being scriptural.

What Says the Scripture?

As we saw in the previous chapter, the first reason for us to reject homosexual marriage is because God says it's wrong. Let us go into more depth regarding what the Bible has to say on the issue.

One homosexual leader wanted to see me recently, and I met with him. Toward the end of the meeting, he said something that was the most astonishing thing I think I have ever heard on the subject. He said that the Bible nowhere ever even mentions homosexuality. Unfortunately, we were just about through with our interview, and I did not have the chance to discuss with him what the Scriptures say about the subject.

My guess is that he would argue that the Bible never condemns homosexuality because the word *homosexuality* itself wasn't coined until the late nineteenth century.[2] Yet the practice existed before that. It certainly existed in biblical times and is clearly condemned by the Scriptures—although you'll never see it condemned by that term—how could it be? This is just semantic gymnastics. This reminds me of those who deny the doctrine of the Trinity since the word is not found in the Bible. The word isn't, but the concept certainly is—veiled in the Old Testament and revealed in the New (e.g., Matt. 28:19).

Here are a few of the references on homosexuality in the Scriptures. In Leviticus 20:13 we read:

> *If a man lies with a male as with a woman, both of them have committed an abomination; they shall surely be put to death; their blood is upon them.*[3]

Dear friends, if lying with mankind as a man lies with womankind is not referring to homosexuality, pray tell me what it is talking about. I haven't a clue if that is not what it means. Furthermore, we read in the New Testament, in Romans 1:26-28, about the plunge of man into the depths of depravity.

> *For this reason God gave them up to dishonorable passions. For their women exchanged natural relations for those that are contrary to nature; and the men likewise gave up natural relations with women and were consumed with passion for one another, men committing shameless acts with men and receiving in themselves the due penalty for their error. And since they*

did not see fit to acknowledge God, God gave them up to a debased mind to do what ought not to be done.

Indeed, what could be clearer than that? In 1 Corinthians 6:9-10 (NIV) we read: "Do not be deceived: Neither the sexually immoral nor idolaters nor adulterers nor male prostitutes nor homosexual offenders [nor others] . . . will inherit the kingdom of God." The Greek word translated as "homosexual offenders" is *arsenokoites*, taken from two Greek words: *arsen*, "male" and *coitus*, "copulation." The term means exactly and precisely "male intercourse." It says nothing about attitude or lust at all. It is the act that is condemned—and those that do it. It says they shall not inherit the kingdom of God.

Note well: Neither adulterers nor fornicators nor homosexuals have any inheritance in the kingdom of God. Do not be deceived, though many today are deceived. Thankfully Paul goes on to say, "And such *were* some of you . . ." (1 Cor. 6:11, emphasis added), but they were changed by the power of the gospel.

However, again, some "Christian homosexuals" today are saying that they can remain active in the homosexual lifestyle and still be accepted by God. They are saying that a proper reading of the Bible leads us to the conclusion that it does not condemn this sin.

In a brochure put out by the Metropolitan Community Churches (the homosexual church), they say, "Most importantly, why do all the other passages of Scripture referring to this account [of the overthrow of Sodom and Gomorrah] fail to raise the issue of homosexuality?"[4] One thing I found about their literature, they seem to be willing to say anything they want, whether it is true or not, I suppose just to deceive the gullible and those who are ignorant.

Well, is it true that none of the other scriptural passages raise the issue of homosexuality? Some of them didn't simply because the term *sodomite* had become such a byword that everybody knew what it was. So if I talk about a person being guilty of sodomy, I don't have to explain the word every time I use it. People know what I am talking about.

But listen to Jude in the NIV: "In a similar way, Sodom and Gomorrah and the surrounding towns gave themselves up to sexual immorality and perversion. They serve as an example of those who suffer the punishment of eternal fire" (v. 7).

No inheritance in the kingdom of God . . . the punishment of eternal fire. Do not be deceived. My friends, the teaching of Scripture could not be clearer. I remember twenty or so years ago somebody asked me if I thought homosexuality was a sin. I said, "Friend, if the Bible does not teach that sodomy or homosexuality is a sin, it doesn't teach that anything is a sin." It could not, in my opinion, be any clearer than it is.

What is the response of homosexuals and lesbians to anyone who says that homosexuality is a sin? They simply say this person is filled with hate; he or she is a homophobe; he or she hates homosexuals. Someone said this is like the Surgeon General's putting this warning on each package of cigarettes: "Warning: Smoking may be dangerous to your health." What did this prove? It proved only that the Surgeon General was a smokophobe and that he hated everyone who smoked cigarettes.

That is perfectly logical—or is it the logic of the reprobate mind? It is ridiculous. Of course, the above conclusion is not true. The Surgeon General is concerned for smokers.

But as we'll see in the next chapter, a study by the Family Research Institute revealed that the average homosexual male's life is forty-two years, whereas the average married heterosexual man's life is seventy-four years. With lesbians, it is forty-four years, whereas with married heterosexual women, it is seventy-nine years. These people are losing almost half of their life, and if they don't come to Christ, they are losing eternal life forever. Should we not be concerned for them? Should we not warn them?

Love the Sinner—Hate the Sin

What should be the attitude of a Christian? We are to love homosexuals and lesbians. For two thousand years it has been the Christian position that we are to love the sinner but hate the sin. Now, I think robbery is a terrible sin, and I hate it. I think rape is a terrible sin, and I hate it. I think the same thing about murder and many other sins. But that doesn't mean I hate the people who do them. I have counseled with people who have done all of those things. I have prayed for them, and I have witnessed to them. I don't hate them.

I don't hate homosexuals, nor can you. Let me say this: A study of 1 John makes it abundantly clear that we must not hate anyone. If we say we are the sons of God, a God who is a God of love, we can't hate people. Vengeance belongs to the Lord, not to us. We are to love the sinner, though we hate the sin. This has always been my attitude toward them. But that does not mean that we lose all moral discernment and proclaim that what they do is perfectly OK.

As I say, I have counseled many of them. I have known homosexuals who have come out of the homosexual lifestyle. I have known those who are struggling in their efforts to try to overcome it. I have known those who are in it and want to stay there. But I have prayed for them all, and so must we all. These are people who desperately need our prayers.

We must pray that God in His mercy will set them free. But, of course, they would have people believe today that they can't be set free, that their "orientation" is something they are born with, and there is nothing they can do about it. Well, my friends, nothing could be further from the truth.

"D.D. Up"—"D.D. Down"

One of the goals of the gay agenda is "D.D. Up" and "D.D. Down." You have probably never heard of those things, so let me explain them. "D.D. Down" means "defining deviancy down." The late Daniel Patrick Moynihan, in his study on this, shows that when deviancy becomes prevalent in a society, societies tend to define deviancy down so they can live with it. Otherwise it becomes too uncomfortable to know there are that many perverts of whatever kind who are living around you.[5] So the American Psychiatric Society defined it down until it became normalcy.

What is "D.D. Up" (defining deviancy up)? It is taking the other side that has always been known as normal and defining that up into deviancy. You say, "Well, that's ridiculous." Listen to Dr. Charles Krauthammer, who says:

> One way is denial: defining real deviancy down creates the pretense that deviancy has disappeared because it has been redefined as normal. Another strategy is distraction: defining deviancy up creates brand-new deviances that we can now go off and fight. That distracts us from real deviancy and gives us the feeling that, despite the murder and mayhem and madness around us, we are really preserving and policing our norms.[6]

So the deviate is declared normal, and the normal is unmasked as deviant. Do you know who the new deviants are? Heterosexuals, family members, fathers, ministers, anyone who says that homosexuality is wrong or sinful. In this process they have now gone so far as to define homosexual deviancy down to normalcy. Some psychologists and psychiatrists have, through therapy, helped homosexuals who have come and said they want to be restored to a heterosexual lifestyle. But attempts are being made to have those therapists declared unethical. Militant homosexuals have a vested interest in their claim that these doctors are abusing psychiatry. So now these therapists are becoming the deviants.

In a letter to the *New York Times*, Dr. Richard Isay, one of the most prominent spokesmen of the group who oppose therapy to help homosexuals *out* of the lifestyle, wrote that

> . . . homophobia—the irrational fear and hatred of homosexuals—is a psychological abnormality. Those afflicted should be quarantined and denied employment.[7]

You just heard a bit of "D.D. Up." You see, the problem isn't homosexuality any more. We have a new deviancy: homophobia. Those who think in this way are the deviants. They are irrational; they are the psychological abnormalities. Homophobia, Isay says, is a psychological abnormality and those afflicted should be quarantined [that's D.D. *Way Up*] and denied employment. That is what they are trying to do to these psychotherapists and psychologists who are trying to help homosexuals toward normalcy.

When there was a great movement in the north to oppress and suppress all statements that slavery was wrong, Abraham

Lincoln was asked what he thought about this and what it would take to satisfy them. He said:

> This and this only [will satisfy them]: cease to call slavery wrong, and join them in calling it right. And this must be done thoroughly—done in acts as well as in words. Silence will not be tolerated.

Senator Stephen Douglas had attempted to pass a new sedition law that would have declared that anyone who said that slavery was wrong had committed a crime. But today we have hate crime bills, and a person can be convicted for what he thinks, if someone decides that is hateful.

Homosexual demonstrators in a recent protest against Coral Ridge Presbyterian Church were carrying signs with the words, "Stop the Hate," "Stop the Hate," "Stop the Hate." But they didn't mention the fact that they have threatened me, saying they were going to blow me up with dynamite, saying they were going to throw AIDS-infected blood in my face.

They didn't tell about the church in San Francisco where the pastor took a stand against them. They fired gunshots through the window of that pastor's home; they tried to firebomb his church.

They didn't tell about the Wednesday evening prayer meeting when homosexuals, shouting obscenities, gathered around the church and threw stones and eggs and vegetables at the people coming to church.

They didn't tell about grabbing the preacher's wife and picking her up bodily to carry her away—only the groundskeeper was able to grab her arm and pull her into the church—very reminiscent of Sodom, would you not say?

They didn't tell how they banged upon the locked doors of a church and took the lawn furniture and beat upon the doors crying out, "We want your children. We want your children."

They carried "Stop the Hate" signs against us, and I have only tried to help them. You don't help people by telling them that cigarette smoking is good for their health. A lot of tobacco addicts don't like to be told that it is wrong, that it is hurtful, that it is dangerous, that it is going to kill them. There are probably few people who don't have loved ones they have tried to dissuade from smoking. Is it because you hate them? No. It is because you love them. Not because you are a smokophobe.

There are people who kill homosexuals—some of the black-jacket guys with chains around their waists who ride around in motorcycle gangs, some of the rednecks, some people who are vile and blasphemous and profane. They love to crack homosexuals' heads and sometimes do. Homosexuals ought to go to a big mass meeting of motorcycle gangs and carry their signs if they want to see some hate. They wouldn't have to worry about AIDS anymore. They would all be dead that afternoon. They would see hate alive and real. But they don't see any of it from us.

We need to pray for these people. We need to witness to them. We need to do good for them. Did any newspaper mention the fact that on my initiative the church I pastor has given money to help people with AIDS? No, there was no mention of that.

The Homosexual Agenda

One of the leading homosexual magazines nationally, *The Advocate*, has run full-page pictures that include renderings of Christ with male and female genitalia, declaring that Christ was homosexual. They have produced motion pictures with that theme, as well as all kinds of vile homoerotic art, depicting Jesus Christ and making Him into a homosexual. *The Advocate* (December 13, 1994) had on its front cover the question, "Is God Gay?" D.D. up, D.D. down.

So, from them we are going to find that homosexuals are normal, and Christ was a homosexual, and God is homosexual, and it is you readers of this book who are the deviates, you people who are the abnormal, you people who should be confined. Does that remind you of what was done in the Soviet Union to people who felt that Communism was sinful and wrong? They were sent to psychiatric wards. A lot of them came out saying, "Oh, yes, Uncle Joe Stalin is wonderful. Communism is great." It is amazing what reeducation can do.

Conclusion

America is being conned, dear friends, and the consequences are serious. Sigmund Freud said that if you remove a public prohibition against homosexuality, it will tend to increase in any culture. That is exactly what we have been doing and what we are doing. May God give us the wisdom to wake up while we have time.

We should pray for those who are in the bondage of sin, as I have prayed for many of them, that God would open their eyes. May they see that they are losing much of their life here, that they are missing out on far greater joys, and most of all, that without Christ they are going into everlasting punishment. May God save this nation. May He change the hearts of people and open the eyes of His followers and help us to deliver this nation back to Him.

6

Homosexuality's Deadly Lifestyle

Do not be deceived:
God is not mocked, for whatever one sows,
that will he also reap.

GALATIANS 6:7

Warning: some of the content of this chapter may be offensive and grotesque. Feel free to jump over to the next chapter if you are faint of heart or stomach.

Have you ever noticed the contrast between how society has reacted to the harms of tobacco compared to the harms of homosexuality? Smoking takes years off of your life—even young schoolchildren learn this. But if children are taught anything about homosexuality, it is presented merely as an *alternative* lifestyle. Virtually nothing is said about the enormous risks involved with the homosexual lifestyle.

This chapter will examine some of the devastation that homosexuality brings in its wake. Consider some of the natural consequences to the unnatural acts of homosexuality.

Early Death

Dr. Paul Cameron, head of the Family Research Institute (in Colorado—not to be confused with the Family Research Council in Washington, DC)—holds a Ph.D. from the University of Colorado. He has published over fifty articles in the recognized scientific press, including the esteemed journal *OMEGA*. He points out that the "average homosexual lifespan is somewhere in the late thirties, early forties for gays. Somewhere from early to middle forties for lesbians."[1] He pored through approximately seven thousand obituaries from eighteen different homosexual publications all over the country. "What we found was this: for gays, if they died of AIDS, the average age of death was 39. If they didn't die of AIDS, their average age of death was still very young, about 42. For lesbians, it ran at 44."[2]

That's an amazing contrast when you consider that the average lifespan for heterosexual men is seventy-three years, for women seventy-seven. That means both men and women who choose the homosexual lifestyle lose, on average, thirty to thirty-five years of life, nearly half a lifetime.

Former Secretary of Education Bill Bennett, author of the *Book of Virtues*, contrasted tobacco use with promiscuous homosexuality: "So what does smoking do to your life? . . . Smoking takes six to seven years off your life. Very important, very serious; we should address that. Promiscuous male homosexuality takes maybe 20 to 30 years off your life."[3] He goes on to point out that we need to be honest about the dangers of this lifestyle: "One of the difficulties in this whole issue is that people have been less than candid, have been afraid to talk frankly about the costs of the promiscuous homosexual lifestyle. . . . The Centers for Disease Control in Atlanta have pointed out in interviews (through the interview process) that a typical, active male homosexual might have two to three hundred partners a year. . . . The biggest problem faced by promiscuous homosexuals in this country is devastation. It's not discrimination; it's devastation. It's death. It's disaster."[4]

How many people do you know personally who have died? As we get older, obviously that number grows. As a pastor, I have buried many congregation members. But returning to my question, how many people do *you* know personally who have died? Let me make an additional qualification: When you were thirty-five, how many people did you know personally who had died? Unless that was during wartime, I imagine the number would be relatively small. Listen to what one ex-gay, who was about age thirty-five, told our television audience: "At this point in my life, there have been at least 94 people that I know who have died of AIDS—personal friends in the past three years."[5]

Reaping What We Have Sown

What has the sexual revolution, with its acceptance of homosexuality and its promotion of promiscuity, brought us? Beyond the psychological and sociological damage, today twenty-six STDs (sexually transmitted diseases) are epidemic in this population. In fact, one in five Americans has some type of viral STD. According to a study by the Alan Guttmacher Institute, fifty-six million Americans are "infected with a sexually transmitted viral disease like herpes or hepatitis B."[6] The tragedy is that while such viral infections can be controlled, they can't be cured, and they often recur.

A few years ago the former Surgeon General of the United States, David Satcher, reported that some twelve million

Americans are infected by sexually transmitted diseases each year.[7] Worldwide there are more than one hundred million cases of gonorrhea alone. In addition, there are cases of syphilis, chlamydia, herpes (millions of people have that), as well as the dreaded AIDS and twenty-one other horrible sexually transmitted diseases.

So maybe God isn't such a killjoy after all by forbidding sex outside of marriage. And maybe every good gift and every perfect gift does come down from above, and not up from beneath with a hook in it and Satan at the other end of the line.

Homosexuality and AIDS

In the late 1980s, we were warned that AIDS was going to break out and overtake the heterosexual population in America. That did not happen. In the United States, HIV and AIDS are still largely homosexual diseases. In Africa, AIDS appears to be more of a heterosexual disease, but that's what happens when widescale promiscuity is coupled with poor hygienic conditions. Sexual promiscuity—whether homosexual or heterosexual—exacts a price.

The Family Research Council has put together a very helpful book, drawing only from secular, widely accepted sources, such as the Centers for Disease Control (the CDC) of Atlanta. This book is called *Getting It Straight* and was written by Peter Sprigg and Timothy Dailey. They point out that homosexuals in America still represent the greatest population with HIV infection. This is because of unhealthy sexual practices. "The high rates of HIV infection among homosexual men are largely due to two behavioral factors—the practice of anal intercourse, which facilitates the transfer of the virus far more easily than vaginal intercourse, and the practice of having sexual relations with multiple sex partners, which multiplies the opportunities for both acquiring and transmitting HIV."[8]

We cannot deal with the specifics of what so many homosexuals actually do. It is too gross. Yet we should at least have a glimpse of some of their practices to understand why homosexuality is killing off so many of them prematurely.

Coauthor Jerry Newcombe will never forget what he was once told by the doctor emeritus in charge of the emergency room of a major hospital in one of our thriving metropolises. The doctor said, in a virtual whisper, "I can't tell you how many times on a Friday and Saturday night, I've seen young men rushed into the emergency room who have rectums that look like raw hamburger meat."

No wonder they get AIDS and Hepatitis-B and all sorts of infectious diseases. As Lorraine Day, M.D., former Chief of Orthopedic Surgery at San Francisco General Hospital, once put it: "Nature said 'exit,' not 'enter.'"[9] In fact, she writes with brutal candor, "Brutal anal sex, 'fisting,' or the use of mechanical sexual aids such as dildos or vibrators produce tears and lacerations of the rectum throughout which infected semen and pathogenic organisms can and will enter the bloodstream. Blood and fecal matter sometimes find their way into the abdominal cavity through injuries. Colitis, a severe inflammation of the mucous membrane of the colon, is not uncommon among gays."[10]

In good conscience, she cannot give the homosexual lifestyle a clean bill of health: "It has been my observation during 15 years as a doctor in one of the world's most-frequented trauma hospitals that much of gay sex is of the harmful, sadistic and/or masochistic variety. Gays hurt each other. They also hurt themselves."[11]

Furthermore, Dr. Stanley Monteith points out that a high percentage of homosexuals engage in something particularly dangerous—rimming: "Rimming is simply licking in and around your partner's anus. And it involves actually placing your tongue into the anus, and you couldn't do this without some ingestion of feces."[12]

Bob Knight of the Culture and Family Institute of Washington, DC, remarks: "We're talking about using parts of the human body that were never designed for sexual activity. You're talking about high bacteria levels in certain areas of the body that just lend themselves to sexually transmitted diseases and other diseases, like gay bowel syndrome, which is a collection of intestinal parasites. You can only get it through this type of activity."[13]

Other Diseases, Beyond AIDS

It isn't just HIV-infection or AIDS that afflicts homosexuals. They are vulnerable to a host of other infectious STDs as well. The Centers for Disease Control note: "Several recent reports have documented alarming increases in sexually transmitted infection rates among men who have sex with men (MSM), and a corresponding decline in safer sex practices. After years of successful prevention efforts, this trend may portend a resurgence of HIV infection in the MSM community."[14]

Furthermore, Sprigg and Dailey of the Family Research Council observe that homosexuals often acquire HPV, Human Papillomavirus: "More than twenty types of HPV are incurable STDs that can infect the genital tract of both men and women.

Most HPV infections are subclinical or asymptomatic, with only one in a hundred people experiencing genital warts."[15] The *Washington Blade,* a leading homosexual newspaper, reports on homosexuals and HPV-infection rates: "A San Francisco study of gay and bisexual men revealed that HPV infection was almost universal among HIV-positive men, and that 60 percent of HIV-negative men carried HPV."[16]

Drug Abuse

While AIDS is a primary cause of death among homosexuals, drug abuse is another problem. Rev. David Foster is well acquainted with the homosexual lifestyle. He once was gay. He was even a male prostitute in Hollywood. He got bit parts during the day as an aspiring actor, and he "turned tricks" in the night. He said this about substance abuse and "the lifestyle":

> Drugs and alcohol are ever present in the homosexual community, at much larger numbers than you find in the heterosexual community. Because in homosexuality, you have a neurosis, you have a neurotic behavior. You have people behaving in ways, for the most part, they don't want to behave in. There's a great deal of emotional, internal distress going on, a great deal of internal pain going on. And so they have to medicate that pain with drugs and alcohol.[17]

One former homosexual points out: "I know many friends that would take horse tranquilizers, at least four or five within a night, on top of taking several other types of barbiturates and at least a bottle of vodka or something throughout the evening—to the point that they would be almost comatose. And this was something I would see on an every night basis."[18]

In his book *Life Outside,* homosexual writer Michelangelo

Signorile confirms the prominence of drugs in the gay lifestyle. He talks about "the international circuit of gay dance parties that take place throughout the year in various cities around the country and around the world. Thousands of men travel to them . . . and the events often turn into several days of partying. Recreational drug use is rampant and almost universal among attendees."[19] In a chapter comparing the gay lifestyle to a religion, he gives further confirmation of the heavy use of drugs in the homosexual lifestyle:

> Gyms are the cult's temples. Nightclubs and sex clubs, its shrines. And the drugs—whether they are the steroids and other compounds many men use to transform their physical bodies, or the Special K, Ecstasy, cocaine, and crystal meth many use to alter their minds—are the mystical elixirs and potions that will take us to a higher place where all is well and where we will bond with one another's souls.[20]

Domestic Violence

Domestic violence is also a problem with homosexual couples. Dr. Paul Cameron says, "Domestic violence, according to Susan Holt, the director of the Gay and Lesbian Center for Domestic Violence in Los Angeles—that's the L.A. gay and lesbian center— she said it's the third leading cause of injury and death in the homosexual community, behind AIDS and substance abuse. The rates of domestic violence among homosexual men exceed those, from the studies we have among married people, by a factor of at least five to six or seven times. Lesbians, somewhere around 8-10 times. As a matter of fact, it looks like lesbian partnerships have the highest rate of domestic violence on the planet."[21]

When you see the early death rates of homosexuals, it is

understandable because of the infectious diseases so many of them acquire from their unhealthy lifestyle. But why do lesbians have a premature death rate on average? High rates of domestic violence.

A Dangerous Lifestyle

So often we hear about homosexuality in terms of it just being an alternative lifestyle. It's presented like a difference in taste. You prefer cream in your coffee; I prefer mine black. To each his own. Whatever floats your boat. But in this case, it seems safer to say, whatever sinks your boat. Live and let live, some say. But in this case it seems to be, live and let die.

And so Dave Foster, former male prostitute, now Christian minister, says, "It's no wonder that AIDS is predominant in the homosexual culture in America. It's due to the great perversion of homosexual sex; it creates a great deal of shedding of blood, and things like that, that transmits the AIDS virus."[22] Another former gay says this about his former life in a gay hot spot of South Florida: "I've watched men after men after men just go through partners in this community as if it was just changing clothes. And I watch them walk around with sores, and I watch them walking around fading because of the promiscuity."[23]

Do not be deceived—God is not mocked. People are reaping what they have sown. But we're told that there is a solution to the AIDS epidemic—the little rubber savior, the condom. But Bob Knight says, "It's an outrage that young people all over this country are being told a lie. They're being told that if you just use condoms, you'll be safe."[24]

Homosexuals themselves admit that the problem is further complicated by those in their ranks who won't use a condom.

Michelangelo Signorile notes that in "Miami's South Beach, a 1996 study showed that more than 75 percent of gay men surveyed had had unprotected anal sex within the previous year."[25] While a condom is usually safer than no condom, abstinence is the best method to prevent getting an STD.

Conclusion

One last danger to highlight about the homosexual lifestyle is the problem of suicide. Homosexuals have a higher suicide rate than their heterosexual counterparts. Former homosexual Mark Culligan of the Tampa area is now involved in ministry to homosexuals. He says, "If teenagers go into the lifestyle, they're choosing a shorter lifespan, they are choosing a high incidence of drug and alcohol abuse and suicide."[26]

The other side may argue that homosexuals are killing themselves in record numbers because of all the homophobia going on out there. Oh really? Former homosexual Dave Foster disagrees:

> Why are you seeing them kill themselves? It's not because society disapproves. The fact is, that society's approval of homosexuality has sky-rocketed since the 1950's. It increases every year. So what you should see is a decreasing of gay-teen suicide, and what you're actually seeing is a logarithmic increase in gay-teen suicide. It's because society is not being allowed to deliver the message to them that they don't have to be a homosexual, that there is hope for them, that they can change.[27]

That hope for change is extremely important. The gospel of Jesus Christ is the ultimate solution to this problem because Christ can change a person from the inside out. That includes homosexuals and lesbians.

7

Scientific Reasons
Why Homosexuals Aren't
Born That Way

For this reason God gave them up to dishonorable passions.
For their women exchanged natural relations for
those that are contrary to nature;
and the men likewise gave up natural relations
with women. . . .

ROMANS 1:26-27

The cornerstone of the homosexual agenda is the myth that "gays are born that way. They can't help it. They are only living out who they really are." We can't solve the problem of same-sex marriages unless we address this falsehood that lies as a root cause of their movement.

So the next two chapters will set out to explode this myth. First, we will deal with the scientific data. Next we will look at the issue from an anecdotal and personal perspective. In other words, we'll hear from former homosexuals and lesbians who have been freed from that sin through the power of Jesus Christ.

Inherited and Genetic?

"It's in their genes," some say—like eye color or skin tone. But is sexual orientation really predetermined by genetics? Recent media reports have led us to believe that science has indeed found a "gay gene." But a closer look reveals they've proven nothing of the sort.

Family Research Council associates Peter Sprigg and Timothy Dailey, authors of *Getting It Straight: What the Research Shows About Homosexuality*, observe: "The research shows no convincing evidence that anyone is 'born gay' and suggests that homosexuality results from a complex mix of developmental factors."[1]

Within the last decade or so, there have been three studies, widely touted in the media, that supposedly point to a physiological basis for homosexuality.

1) Dr. Simon LeVay's study supposedly found that the brains of homosexuals were different from those of heterosexuals. Specifically, a tiny, tiny portion (about the size of a grain of sand) of the anterior hypothalamus was sometimes, not always, smaller in the cadavers of homosexuals than in the cadavers of heterosexuals.

Spriggs and Dailey point out: "LeVay's study, however, suffered from serious methodological errors, including the failure to adequately identify a control group."[2] And they add, "LeVay, in fact, admitted that his claim of a *correlation* between this brain structure and sexual orientation could not prove *causation,* or even the direction of influence."[3] Not only that, other researchers could not replicate LeVay's findings, and neither could LeVay himself.[4]

2) J. Michael Bailey and Richard C. Pillard conducted a

1991 study of identical twins separated at birth, some of whom went on to become homosexual, even though they were raised in different homes.

Researcher Miron Baron shows the flaw of this study: "The finding that the adoptive brothers of homosexual twins are more prone to homosexuality than the biological siblings suggests that male homosexuality may well be environmental."[5] In other words, the type of home the young person lives in determines his homosexuality, not his genetic makeup.

Dr. William Byne and Dr. Bruce Parsons of Columbia University found another flaw in this study. Spriggs and Dailey sum up Byne's and Parsons' findings: "If homosexuality were a trait determined entirely by a person's genes, one would expect 100 percent of the identical (monozygotic or MZ) twins of homosexuals to also be homosexual. Yet this is not the case; indeed, 'what is most intriguing' about the twins studies to Byne and Parsons 'is the large proportion of MZ twins who were discordant for homosexuality despite sharing not only their genes but also their prenatal and familial environments."[6] This argues for the case that homosexuality is the product of nurture, not nature—the very opposite claim of what Bailey and Pillard claimed.

3) Researcher Dean Hamer supposedly isolated a gay gene, as published in *Science* (July 16, 1993).

Dr. Charles Socarides, author of *Homosexuality: A Freedom too Far*, is a former professor of clinical psychology at Albert Einstein College of Medicine in New York. When asked what Hamer's report really says, Socarides answered: "1) That researchers were looking for a gay gene. 2) That they didn't find one. 3) But they may have found a neighborhood where they can keep looking for one. 4) That not everyone who's gay has that gene."[7] Because of all this, Dr. Socarides calls Hamer's findings "pseudo-science."[8]

Hamer's research has not been successfully duplicated. Sprigg and Dailey state: "The 1999 study in *Science* by [George] Rice, et al., attempted without success to duplicate Hamer's findings."[9] Rice and others say, "These results do not support an X-linked gene underlying male homosexuality."[10]

Therefore, Sprigg and Dailey sum up: "To date, all theories regarding the existence of a 'gay gene' remain unsubstantiated. However, some researchers suggest that genetics may play an indirect role through the presence of certain temperamental traits that increase the likelihood that certain individuals will experience same-sex attractions or come to identify themselves as homosexual."[11]

The media contributes to this confusion. The day of the supposed finding, the headlines shouted: "SCIENTISTS DISCOVER GAY GENE!" The subsequent debunking of the alleged gay gene was buried somewhere in a follow-up story on page D-18 or wherever—in small print, no less.

Drs. William Byne and Bruce Parsons of Columbia wrote a scholarly paper, "Human Sexual Orientation: The Biologic Theories Reappraised." They conclude that there is no evidence at present to substantiate a biological theory—though the press, of course, fastens upon these things in their desire to make money by selling papers and in their zeal tragically come down on the wrong side of the moral fence, as they seem to do repeatedly. Byne and Parsons observe, "Finally, political arguments have been offered in favor of biologic causation. It has been suggested that if sexual orientation is largely a biologic phenomenon, 'society would do well to reexamine its expectations of those who cannot conform'; and writing in the 'Opinions and Editorials' pages of the *New York Times* (December 17, 1991:19), Bailey and Pillard stated: "If true, a biological explanation is good news for homosexuals and their advocates.' However, political arguments have no impact on biologic realities, including the extent of genetic or hormonal influences on the emergence of sexual orientation."[12] In short, some researchers—virtually all of whom are homosexual, by the way—are putting politics over science and therefore hyping their "findings," which are neither conclusive nor capable of being replicated.

Thus, all of these studies supposedly pointing to a biological basis for homosexuality (again, all by homosexual scientists) are flawed. Dr. G. van den Aardweg, a Dutch psychiatrist, in his book says that "although there have been many reports during the last 50 years of biological differences in homosexuals, on closer inspection or replication, such studies could not be confirmed."[13]

Discredited Science

One psychiatrist who actually works with homosexuals—helping them out of the lifestyle—is Dr. Richard Fitzgibbons, the director of a counseling service in the Philadelphia area. He notes, "There is no research supporting a genetic basis of homosexuality. The work of [Chandler] Burr has been discredited by *Scientific American*, the brain study of Simon LeVay has been discredited. They're desperate to find the biological causes. There are none."[14]

James Mallory, M.D., is the director of the Atlanta Counseling Center. He points out: "If they can identify a gene that is more commonly seen in homosexuals what they're going to be finding is a gene that produces some sort of trait that makes them a little more vulnerable to become a homosexual—such as being rejected by peers. . . . The idea though that they're going to come up with a gene that is causal is not going to occur."[15]

Dr. Mallory feels that homosexuality is analogous to alcoholism. There may be some biological traits that contribute to the problem, but certainly there is personal responsibility involved. The offender has a choice in the matter:

> There's a good analogy between alcoholism and homosexuality. And they've done exhaustive, genetic studies on alcoholism, and there is clearly some sort of a genetic vulnerability. But again it's not causal; it just ups the risk factor that if the person drinks, they will become alcoholic. Homosexual behavior is the cause of homosexuality just like drinking alcohol is the cause of alcoholism. As with alcoholism, many therapists agree that certain physical and psychological traits may make a person more vulnerable to homosexuality, and those temptations may become even stronger after a traumatic experience—like rejection—or sexual abuse.[16]

In his book *When Wish Replaces Thought*, Steven Goldberg says, concerning a genetic cause, "Virtually all of the evidence argues against there being a determinative physiological causal factor, and I know of no researcher who believes that such a determinative factor exists."[17]

Again, there are factors that may play a predisposing but not a determinative role. People have different kinds of personalities. Some people are very aggressive. Some people are very shy. Some people have predisposing tendencies toward alcoholism or hotheadedness. But that does not mean we should, therefore, put our imprimatur upon those things as being all right.

Homosexual activists will say, "Well, some animals are homosexual." Perhaps, but there are some animals that eat their own young; so I guess we shouldn't complain when people do that. There are obviously animals that are cannibalistic in other ways as well. Some animals destroy all kinds of other animals. So, therefore, all of those things should be perfectly all right, if that is the kind of logic one wants to use.

The American Psychiatric Association

But, you say, didn't the American Psychiatric Association take homosexuality off the deviant lists some years ago and declare that it was no longer pathological? That's correct. They did. But how about the rest of the story? We now know that the man most responsible in pushing for that change has come out of the closet and revealed himself to be a homosexual. In fact, he has written a book entitled *The Joy of Gay Sex* and a new book entitled *The New Joy of Gay Sex*.[18] We would list for you the Table of Contents to that second book except we would be too embarrassed. The chapter titles are too kinky and perverted.

A recent president of the American Psychiatric Association was "outed" several years ago at the association's annual meeting by a group of homosexuals. Do you know what it means to be "outed"? That means other homosexuals push you out of the closet when you don't want to come out. He would neither deny nor affirm the accusations, but the homosexuals who knew him more intimately affirmed just what he was.

Let's dig deeper as to why the American Psychiatric Association decided to remove homosexuality from their list of mental disorders in 1973. Dr. Charles Socarides witnessed the APA's decision firsthand. He says, "The change in the diagnosis was strictly a political one. There was never any investigation of the scientific evidence for that. No scientific evidence was produced. A board of trustees heavily weighted towards gay activism took charge and removed it without scientific study whatsoever. No scientific study had been done. And nor had the experts in the field—like Irving Bieber, myself, and other people—never were we asked for our opinion. It was just rammed through without scientific study and without evidence."[19] Socarides sums up: "The organization was under political assault by gay activists—some of them members of the APA itself. It was easier for the leadership to switch than fight."[20]

Another eyewitness to the change within the APA is Dr. Mallory. He points out: "The fact is, back in the late sixties this started from a very small minority of homosexuals, within the APA and without, who had begun to lobby to get rid of that as a diagnosis. I was at a meeting in San Francisco around '68 or '69 and there were quite a few people with placards marching around our meetings and so forth. And then in 1973, they held a referendum to see if the psychiatrists would agree to delete it from the Diagnostic Manual and only twenty-five percent of the psychiatrists voted. Of those twenty-five percent, three out of five said, Delete it from the diagnostic manual. So that means that [the vote of only] fifteen percent of the psychiatrists resulted in homosexuality being deleted from the diagnostic manual. And there was such a furor from the majority of psychiatrists over them having done that."[21]

This change did not occur without a fight. "We were very concerned. We went down to the APA headquarters and protested, and we were given short shrift," says Dr. Socarides, who objected to the decision because it was not based on science but on politics. "We were given five minutes each. I outlined for example the social consequences, which have now appeared in their full force for a number of years now."[22] Who could have known that within thirty years of that decision, we would be battling same-sex marriage?

Meanwhile, an American Psychiatric Association survey of thirty-four countries reveals that their psychiatric associations declare homosexuality to be either pathological, mental illness, or sexual deviation,[23] and that our psychiatric association has become a laughing stock, having abandoned scientific principle for political correctness. Homosexuals have often gotten themselves in positions of influence and have moved society in their direction.

According to a 1992 study of 125 psychiatric associations around the world, all but three still consider homosexuality a mental illness or a sexual deviation. That means that U.S. psychiatrists are joined only by Denmark and South Africa in their liberal stance. According to Dr. Socarides, this radical stance has caused a radical change in our nation: "This omission of a diagnosis was a Trojan horse under which individuals throughout this country, gay activists, would begin to change—how people behaved, what they thought of same sex contacts, how children were brought up, sex education in the schools, sex education in general, would be changed radically. And that's what happened unfortunately."[24]

Perhaps the worst result of both the APA's decision and the "born gay" philosophy in general is the fact that many homosexuals who *want* help are often discouraged from seeking it. Instead of therapists being able to help them, this in effect slammed the door in the faces of those who were seeking help.

Dr. Mallory says, "There are a lot of studies out that show 66% of homosexuals that desire to change have done so. And yet there are a lot of psychiatrists who will not treat a person who comes in saying, 'I'm a homosexual, and I don't like it and I want to change,' and they will not treat them. And there are some in fact who will tell them that you just need to adjust to the fact that you're a homosexual, and I'll help you adjust to it."[25]

To be involved in this type of therapy—moving individuals out of homosexuality—that Dr. Mallory, Dr. Socarides, Dr. Fitzgibbons, and others are engaged in is very much swimming against the tide. Dr. Fitzgibbons observes, "This takes a great deal of courage to really pursue the treatment of homosexuality. You have to have a great love for truth. Your love for truth has to be greater than your concern for what your colleagues think."[26]

And who loses? Society, the children, but also homosexuals themselves. They shorten their lifespan and then—unless they repent and accept Jesus Christ as their Redeemer—plunge into hell. As Dr. Socarides notes, "They required our compassion; they did not require our embracing a sexual deviation as normal."[27]

Causes of Homosexuality

So what causes, or can contribute to, the rise of homosexuality?

Dr. Fitzgibbons says a multitude of factors can lead a person to become a homosexual or a lesbian, but virtually all of them get back to what happened when the subject was a small child: "There are countless numbers of articles pointing to significant emotional trauma in early childhood in those with homosexual attractions. That is, gender-identity disorders. I had a patient the other day; he never liked his body from an early age. Always craved the masculinity of another. He craved the body of another. That's why there is such rampant promiscuity. There is this emptiness in their masculinity, and they want to obtain it by someone else. Second in males is a distant father relationship, and they get a negative view of one's body. And women, the number one [cause] is a mistrust of men. It's different than men. The mistrust of men in women is based usually on having a very difficult father relationship—also being sexually abused by other men or by being hurt by other men. So a lot of women are afraid to open up their hearts to males and subsequently back into homosexual relationships by default."[28]

One man who has also experienced a lot of success in treating homosexuals is psychologist Dr. Joseph Nicolosi, clinical director of the Thomas Aquinas Clinic in Encino, California. Like the other therapists, Dr. Nicolosi is hated by the homosexual activists because he has been so successful in helping homosexuals change to heterosexuals, through what he calls "reparative therapy."[29] The activists hate these counselors because the success of their work disproves a couple of their sacred theories—that you're born that way and that you can never change.

Dr. Nicolosi says that psychologists from an earlier era (even Sigmund Freud) categorized homosexuality as a disorder, but a disorder that can be treated:

Anna Freud in the early forties—the daughter of Sigmund Freud—reported the healing of three homosexuals based on the idea that they were trying to connect with the masculine that they never had within themselves. Who reads about this? This is something I discovered in the literature.[30]

Dr. Nicolosi, president of NARTH (National Association for Research and Treatment of Homosexuality) and the editor of the helpful *NARTH Bulletin*, cites another famous psychologist in times past who found psychological problems that caused homosexuality:

> Irving Bieber did a classic study with over a hundred men in psychoanalysis. Repeatedly, statistically, he found that they had a poor relationship with their father. And I see this time and time again. But all this information is politically incorrect; so it's being buried, and people are just believing that homosexuals are born this way.[31]

Fallout from the Feminist Movement

One of the reasons many young males have turned to homosexuality is gender confusion. Much of the blame has to be laid at the feet of the feminist movement.

When women ceased to be caregivers and full-time mothers, when being a wife was not an occupation anymore, and homemaking was for idiots who could not do anything else, what were the males to do? They were not needed anymore, no more than "a fish needs a bicycle." They were not to be protectors and providers. We went from "Father Knows Best" to "Dad's-an-idiot" sitcoms. (Consider Homer Simpson as an example.) No wonder our males are confused about who they are supposed to be.

In his article "Parental Background of Male Homosexuals and Heterosexuals," Marvin Siegelman says that it has been a repeated finding—really, as long as psychology has been a discipline—that dominating mothers and weak fathers contribute to the development of homosexuality: "Freud (1916) described the mothers of homosexuals as excessively loving and their fathers as retiring or absent. [Wilhelm] Stekel (1930) noted strong, dominant mothers and weak fathers. In 1936, [L.] Terman and [Walter] Miles found the mothers of homosexuals to be especially demonstrative, affectionate, and emotional, while the fathers were typically unsympathetic, autocratic, or frequently away from home."[32]

Family dynamics—a detached father combined with a dominating mother—appears to be the leading cause of homosexuality in boys.[33] Dominating women and women's libbers, take note: When you put on the pants in the family, you may put your son in a skirt.

But Dad abdicating his role in the household is also a huge contributing factor. Stating it positively, Dr. Charles Socarides notes: "Given a good father-son relationship, no boy develops a homosexual pattern."[34] That is such an important observation that we will repeat it in bold letters. **Dr. Charles Socarides notes: "Given a good father-son relationship, no boy develops a homosexual pattern."**

The good news of all this is that homosexuals and lesbians *can* change. Many do. Many work through reparative therapy. Many change through the power of the gospel, working in conjunction with a Christian ex-gay group. But they have to want to change. This is like the old joke—how many psychologists does it to take to change a light bulb? Only one, but the light bulb has to *want* to change.

Conclusion

Jeff Johnson is a former homosexual and is now a therapist who helps men and women out of homosexuality. He says, "The biggest problem I have with any of those studies [on a supposed biological basis for homosexuality] is that they take away our free will. They reduce us to mechanistic beings who are drawn to our genes, and God said we're more than that. I never bought into the idea that I was gay or that that was my identity. My identity is as a man; my identity is as a son of God; as one of His creations. My identity is as a heterosexual man; that is what God intended me to be."[35]

In the next chapter we will hear from people like Jeff Johnson. Those who at one time embraced the "gay" lifestyle but have been freed by the power of Christ.

8

Confessions of Ex-gays
and Ex-lesbians

*And such were some of you. But you were washed,
you were sanctified, you were justified in the name of the
Lord Jesus Christ and by the Spirit of our God.*

1 CORINTHIANS 6:11

Sy Rogers was so immersed in the homosexual lifestyle that
for about a year and a half, he dressed up and lived as a
woman. He worked in a clerical job in an office in the
Washington, DC, area, and it was assumed by his employer and
colleagues that he was a woman. He writes: "Achieving much
desired acceptance in my role as a woman, I was considered
attractive and even popular in gay circles."[1] Meanwhile, he was
undergoing the lengthy counseling needed for a sex change oper-
ation at Johns Hopkins Hospital. However, that institution
announced they would no longer perform that procedure.
Through a series of events, Rogers became a Christian and was
freed from his homosexuality and from his desire to dress like a
woman. He got involved with Exodus International and with
helping homosexuals come out of that lifestyle through

Christianity. Today Sy Rogers is married and has children; he helps those who are suffering from sexual brokenness, including homosexuality, through the power of Jesus Christ. Sy Rogers is a great example that gays are not born that way. If they were, how could they change?

In the last chapter, we heard from scientists and psychologists, exploding the myth that homosexuals are born as homosexuals. This chapter is devoted to the personal side of the issue. The following are true testimonials of ex-homosexuals and ex-lesbians. The names have been changed to protect their privacy.

Are homosexuals born that way?

Ben: Most of my life I did feel that I was born this way, I was born gay. I didn't feel that I could change.

Chris: It had started at a very young age. I had always believed that I was born that way.

Tony: I thought this was the way that I was born, and I'll never get out of this. And I'm stuck this way for the rest of my life, and I hate it. And there's no point in living.

What factors cause or contribute to homosexuality?

Tim: When a homosexual neurosis begins, it's not at all sexual. It's purely an emotional need. You generally fail to bond with your father or your father figure in your life, emotionally. And so what's happening is, you're longing for an emotional completion that's not there. And so very early on I had that longing for an emotional completion with another man.

Chris: I had not gotten same-sex love needs met as a child, and I was looking for that. At the age of ten, that became neuroticized.

Ben: If I had had that admiration, if I had that love from my dad and had him there to teach me what it means to be a man, play ball with me or do whatever he needed to do, then I wouldn't have felt those homosexual orientations. All of that would have been fulfilled back at the time that it needed to be.

Dan: When I was about five years old, I was raped by a young teenage boy in our neighborhood, and I really didn't believe at the time I had anybody to talk to about it.

Beth: I was molested as a child by a friend of my brother's when I was ten.

Joe: I was molested when I was around eleven by a good family friend.

Sally: When I was seven years old, I was sexually abused by some members of my family, not my father or my brothers—outside my immediate family—and that happened from the age of seven until I was about fifteen.

Rick: When I was fourteen, I was molested by an older stranger in a public place; and that just kind of said to me that here's someone that's interested in me, and it happens to be a man. There's a possibility that I'm gay.

What are people seeking in the homosexual lifestyle? What did you find there?

Rick: I think I was seeking someone, particularly a male, to say, "You're OK, and I like you the way you are."

Beth: I was seeking love out of the gay lifestyle. I was seeking love and acceptance by other women.

Chris: The first time I ever felt completely accepted and loved was the first time I walked into a homosexual nightclub.

Sally: I was looking for affirmation from my lifestyle as a lesbian.

Robert: You leave your own family; and you get embraced by the homosexual community, and they engulf you as their family.

What was the gay lifestyle like for you?

Rick: For me, most of my sexual encounters were anonymous. I didn't even know the person's name. It was usually a daily occurrence.

Robert: The promiscuity that was involved was so intense.

Joe: Anonymous sex, probably once, twice a week.

Chris: I wasn't sleeping with everybody. I wasn't going and having one-night stands every night. I wasn't very promiscuous, but I did have a lot of partners.

Beth: You could go out to a bar with your girlfriend; and if she sees someone else that is attractive to her, even though you have those emotional ties, she's not necessarily going to be tied to you.

Sally: That relationship that I was in for ten years was very emotionally abusive, physically abusive at times; and it was like living a crisis day in and day out for ten years.

Charles: I went into gay bars. There were thousands of people. There were doctors. There were lawyers. There were priests. There were ministers, and there is excitement there. There is an air of expectancy and running and travel and money and drugs and alcohol. I got into making pornographic films and magazines, and I was in gay body-building contests, and I went to San Francisco and I saw it all.

Tim: I ended up as a male prostitute and probably had over a thousand partners before the Lord saved me.

Jack: On Sunday I was in church, looking all prim and proper, directing the choir. On Monday, I was at park restrooms, looking for sexual hits.

Dan: My entire life seemed to be centered around the sexual aspects of homosexuality.

Chris: My lord at that time, in my opinion, was my sexuality. It defined everything about me—life, my politics, art, and all that stuff.

Do you think that homosexuals are pleased with their lifestyle?

Robert: When I was in the homosexual lifestyle, there were many times and many seasons of fun for me in the homosexual lifestyle. But then there came the larger seasons. Those years it was extremely painful. Painful enough to [consider] suicide.

Charles: When I was involved in the homosexual act, I remember one time especially I was involved in the act; and the thought went through my mind, "How would you like to die now, Charles, and meet your Creator, right now?"

Joe: I was never happy that I was gay, but no one ever offered me a way out.

Sally: I felt totally out of control, and at times I felt as if, if I go any further—I just don't know how far I could carry this rage.

Charles: If you separate them, one on one, there's some very wretched people who are hurting deeply.

Dan: Pain and rejection? All the time—all the time.

Tony: I don't know that anybody's really happy with it, and I don't buy those images [of happy gays]. Because I know too many people who have gone to the gay pride parades, and I know the suffering that they live through Monday through Friday. So I don't believe that those are valid images.

Tim: There's a great deal of emotional, internal distress going on, a great deal of internal pain going on.

Is there a way out?

Charles: Eight years ago I got a phone call. It was from a doctor in Pittsburgh, and I was told that I had the AIDS virus. I remember hanging the phone up; and I went into my bedroom, and I kicked my shoes off. I sat on my bed, and I just wept like a baby. From that day on, it was a struggle—yes—but from that day on, I never engaged in another homosexual act. I never went to another gay bar, and I realized what I had to do. I began reading my Bible again. I began having prayer time.

Tony: I went to sleep one night and was just praying, "Lord, I can't do this anymore." And I closed my eyes, and I saw a vision of the cross, and I saw Jesus on the cross, and I heard that still, small voice again say to me, "Whenever you get tempted to fall, think about the cross and everything I've done for you." And in that moment there was a healing that took place inside of me; I knew that the compulsion was broken; I knew homosexuality was broken. I didn't know how it would all take place and how it would all work out in my life, but it was a moment in time that I knew was the turning point.

Rick: I went to my minister friend and just shared it with him, and that was the beginning of recovery for me. I became accountable to him. If he asked me, "Are you acting on these desires, are you having sex, are you going to the bookstores, are you going to the park?" I could not lie to him.

Ben: God's healing agent is the church and that community and being able to be involved in the church. And that's where you're going to begin walking out of the homosexual orientation because you're going to be finding out that these guys love you because of the fact that you're a brother in Christ.

Sally: I have experienced an incredible rebirth. I feel as if my eyes have opened, and I've been able to see colors that I've never even seen before, that are just so much brighter. God has just given me, truly, a new life, and I know that may be hard for people to believe. I've heard other people talk about this kind of experience. But for me, it really has been an experience of new life, a new start. And I thank God for that.

Can homosexuals and lesbians be totally freed?

Jack: People in our culture do not know that homosexuals and lesbians can change. It is a critical message, an important message, and must be spoken.

Tim: If anybody says that you cannot change from homosexual orientation to heterosexual orientation, they're either ignorant or they're lying.

Ben: I never dreamed that the orientation would go away, that it would change, that it would get me to the point in my life where it's not a temptation anymore. I do know that a person, if they apply themselves, can get out of this. Given the right information, it's never too late to change—because *I* did when I decided that I was not going to be involved in homosexuality anymore.

Charles: As a man thinks, so he is. I cannot take filth into my mind and then expect to be an upright, righteous person. But if I take good into my thinking, and practice that good, I will see the results in my life. I do not walk on water, I am not perfect, but my mind is so totally changed that where I am now, if somebody would have asked me ten years ago of the hope that I now have, and this success I have, I would have told them they were out of their mind.

Robert: As a homosexual, when I laid my head down at night, I had to think about all the shame I felt. I felt, even though I said I was free and was very happy about being gay, there was still a feeling of entrapment. I felt like I had committed myself to something that I really was not sure that I could handle. And because of that, it drew me into a fury of trying to prove myself. And I found that most of my friends were the same way. You had to continuously prove yourself in that lifestyle. And I think about when Christ says that whoever the Son shall set free is free indeed, you know. And when Christ did set me free, I thought, *Wow. Here I am a Christian, and I can truly express myself, and*

I feel no shame, no guilt, no nothing. I would take the worst day as a Christian knowing Jesus Christ rather than the best day without Him.

Ann: There are thousands who have come out of the lifestyle. They're living lives that are glorifying to God. They've left their homosexuality behind and are happy for it. Certainly, there are failures. Anybody who tries to change habits of any kind will go back. People may have a whole series of false starts before they actually connect and get moving.

Jane (wife of Dan): To say that people can't be transformed is to say that God cannot transform people and that's blasphemy. Nothing less.

Tony: 1997 makes fifteen years out of the lifestyle for me. Ten years married with three beautiful children, and I'm just grateful to the Lord and everything that He's done in my life. Because there is hope.[2]

These testimonials are just a taste of the very large but rather unknown ex-gay movement. For the most part, the mainstream media has not pursued this story—except perhaps in the rare case when an ex-gay person falls back into the homosexual lifestyle. That happens, just as saved sinners of all stripes occasionally fall into sin. The key is that they return to Christ. Thankfully, there are thousands and thousands of men and women today who are a part of the official ministry of Exodus and other Christian ministries to homosexuals and lesbians. And who knows how many Christians were once engaged in the homosexual lifestyle and are now free but never went through such programs?

The next time you hear someone say that homosexuals and lesbians are born that way, keep these testimonials in mind. Same-sex marriage is being accepted by some because of the false premise that homosexuals or lesbians are born as homosexuals or lesbians. Ben, Rick, Charles, Sally, and others know firsthand that's not true.

Steps for Change

The people from Exodus International are actively helping homosexuals and lesbians out of this lifestyle. As Thom Rogers, former homosexual, once put it: "We're here to say that if someone is struggling and wanting to come away from homosexuality, we will share with you what we've found. And what we have found, of course, is Jesus Christ."[3]

There are two main steps in overcoming homosexuality. The first is a genuine desire to change. If this is combined with a Christian conversion and the right input (e.g., working with an Exodus group), there is a great chance for success. That's because true freedom, forgiveness, and cleansing are only found in Jesus Christ. Former homosexual Van Craig says:

> I've seen the tremendous amount of hope that is in the Word of God. And the thing that amazes me is that the one place that I have found acceptance, the one place that I have found hope is in the Lord Jesus and in the church now. And truly when the Bible says He is able to do exceedingly abundantly beyond what we think or ask, that is what I am personally experiencing.[4]

Years earlier, Van thought the church was *the last place* where he'd find the answer. He said, "I was rejected by a youth pastor who everything but really threw me out of his office. The poor guy was totally unequipped for everything I came in and dumped on him, although that was pretty soft-core, compared to what came into my life later. I just got a lot of attitudes from my Christian friends and from people in church during that time that were very damaging."[5]

As Christians we need to be careful not to don our pharisaical garbs about this sin (or any other). We really do need to love the sinner, while of course holding out against the sin.

The second step to help homosexuals and lesbians change is to build *nonsexual* friendships with members of the same sex. Josh McDowell points out that close friendships are needed: "not just a ministry friendship, but a personal friendship."[6]

Christian therapist Dr. Elizabeth Moberly has had a lot of success treating homosexuals and lesbians. She says of the cause of homosexuality: "There's a lot of evidence of difficulties in early relationships. The point of therapy is to make good those difficulties."[7] She says, "The boy, let's say, still has an unmet need for his father's love."[8] Homosexuality, then, is the result of unmet needs caused by broken relationships early in life and wrong choices later in life. Says Dr. Moberly, "In reality, it's still the little boy needing his father's love. That's an entirely legitimate need, but it shouldn't be expressed sexually."[9] And how do we help such people? Dr. Moberly notes: "If the churches are willing to drop unhelpful attitudes, hostility or forcing the person in the arms of the opposite sex, if they'll focus instead on constructive same-sex friendships and same-sex counseling, that is going to make a whole lot of difference."[10]

Thus it behooves us, the heterosexual community—especially as Christians—to be a part of the solution and not part of the problem. If you or someone you know is struggling with homosexuality, we highly recommend finding out about the Exodus International affiliate in your area. Their phone number is 407-599-6872, or you can check their web site (www.exodus-international.org).

Conclusion

Look at the brokenness expressed in the above testimonials. Are we as a society willing to put millions of children at risk for this kind of emotional brokenness, not to mention the myriad of diseases, in order to satisfy the whims of the homosexual activists and a few unelected judges?

America is at a crossroads. If we fully embrace same-sex marriage, there will be far more young men and women in our society brought down into the mire of sexual sin. We should listen to what these ex-gays have to say: Don't normalize homosexuality by accepting same-sex marriage.

EPILOGUE

Where Do We Go from Here?

"And who knows whether you have not come to the kingdom for such a time as this?"

ESTHER 4:14

My friend, I believe these are critical days. We are at a crossroads as a nation. We are far down the wrong path. Judges who have skirted over the plain meaning of the Constitution have now found "rights" therein clearly not supported by the text, nor by our history—and certainly not by the Word of God, upon which this nation was founded.

We are in a dangerous time, and many Christians don't even realize it. They don't realize how precarious our religious freedoms are. They don't know what is going on in countries like Canada and Sweden, where it is a hate crime to speak out against homosexuality.

Sound far-fetched? In April 2003 the Canadian parliament passed a measure criminalizing "hate speech" against homosexuals. The law has a religious exemption, but that is little comfort since a Saskatchewan court has found the Bible to be hate literature. It upheld in 2003 a fine against a man who placed a newspaper ad with Bible verses on homosexuality.[1] Also in 2003, Swedish authorities arrested a pastor for "hate speech against homosexuals" after he preached a sermon with biblical references to homosexuality.

For our broadcast, *The Coral Ridge Hour*, coauthor Jerry Newcombe interviewed a pastor in Sweden, Rev. Ingo Sünderland. That pastor said that the church authorities there have so caved into the homosexual agenda that they view what the Bible says on the subject as obsolete, preferring instead modern "science" (but as we've seen, that's just politically correct science). Rev. Sünderland said, "The church says that the Bible has to be interpreted from the new facts we have in the society today and the science."[2] Plans are already in the works to remove references to homosexuality in Bible passages such as Romans 1 and from the lectionary that is used in the churches throughout the country.

He also said, "I'm risking fines and also the right to preach, to be a priest in a Swedish church, because the Swedish church has a line there that says homosexuality is okay."[3] Even if he or someone like him says what the previous chapter discussed—that homosexuality is a sin from which Jesus Christ can deliver individuals—he could be at risk to be fined, lose his job, or even possibly be thrown in jail for "hate speech."

Federal Marriage Amendment

I believe from the bottom of my heart that the time to act is now. Do you remember when all the Jews of Persia and beyond were sentenced to death by order of King Xerxes because he listened to the counsel of the wicked Haman? By the grace of God one woman was able to prevent this: Queen Esther. But initially she did not want to get involved. She knew that if she stood before the king uninvited—which she would have to do to solve this mess—the king could turn down her request and even send her to her death. Nonetheless, her Uncle Mordecai told her that she had to take this stand. He said to her, "For if you keep silent at this time, relief and deliverance will arise for the Jews from another place, but you and your father's house will perish. And who knows whether you have not come to the kingdom for such a time as this?" (Esther 4:14).

Who knows that God hasn't brought you to this place in this country at this time so that you can get involved in this issue?

Many of the leading authorities opposed to same-sex marriage think the best thing to do—although it is certainly not the easiest—is to pass a constitutional amendment that defines marriage as being between one man and one woman. Period.

For many years now, leading conservative legal scholars have been working on the Federal Marriage Amendment, in conjunction with Matt Daniels of the Alliance for Marriage. Included in that list is the Honorable Robert Bork, one of the leading legal minds of our time, who was denied a position on the U.S. Supreme Court because of a vicious campaign of character assassination. Here is the wording of the Federal Marriage Amendment: "Marriage in the United States shall consist only of the union of a man and a woman. Neither this constitution or the constitution of any state, nor state or federal law, shall be construed to require that marital status or the legal incidents thereof be conferred upon unmarried couples or groups."[4] This is also commonly known as the Musgrave Amendment in honor of the Christian Congresswoman, Marilyn Musgrave (R, Colorado), who introduced it in the House.

What's Wrong with Same-Sex Marriage?

We must never forget that the U.S. Supreme Court (in *Lawrence v. Texas,* June 2003) made possible the same-sex marriage decision by the Massachusetts Supreme Court (*Goodridge v. Massachusetts,* November 2003). How? By striking down a law passed by a state legislature (in that case, Texas). The U.S. Congress and thirty-eight states have passed a DOMA (Defense of Marriage Act)—defining marriage as being between one man and one woman. But the U.S. Supreme Court could nullify all these laws by the stroke of a pen and the bang of a gavel.

When we consider the societal ills of abortion, pornography, and the public schools largely becoming "religion-free zones," we must not forget that many of these things go back to decisions by the U.S. Supreme Court. So it is not preposterous to think the U.S. Supreme Court could one day rule in favor of gay marriage.

In fact, it is completely conceivable that a consensus of the current Supreme Court could strike down all the DOMA laws. Listen to what they said when six (out of nine) of them voted to overturn Texas's anti-sodomy statute. This is from *Lawrence v. Texas*:

> The *Casey* decision[5] again confirmed that our laws and tradition afford constitutional protection to personal decisions relating to marriage, procreation, contraception, family relationships, child rearing, and education. . . . Persons in a homosexual relationship may seek autonomy for these purposes, just as heterosexual persons do.[6]

In other words, although the Supreme Court was not ruling whether homosexuals could marry per se, the majority of the members said that homosexuals have the right to marriage. Thus the DOMA laws are not safe from the high court. That is why I support the Federal Marriage Amendment. The goal is to make it impossible for judges to impose gay marriage on the country by judicial fiat.

We no longer seem to be governed by the Constitution and three branches of government. We no longer seem to be "We the People." Things have changed to where we are now "We the Judges." The Constitution is what the judges say it is, and they are finding all sorts of justification for things that contradict the written text and the original intent of the founding fathers. Open up your Constitution, and read Amendments 9 and 14. Those were the justification of *Roe v. Wade*. They mention nothing about the "right to terminate one's pregnancy," "the right to privacy," or the like. The Fourteenth Amendment mentions the "right to life," but the Supreme Court ruled in favor of abortion anyway.

If the Constitution were amended to enshrine the protection of marriage—and take this issue out of the hands of unelected judges, many of whom hold their positions for life—we could go a long way toward solving this mess.

Are "We the People" Apathetic?

Tragically, when I have voiced my opinions to Congressmen and Senators, I have been told that the people don't seem to care. They have told me that people are not burning up their phones or sending them many e-mails or letters about this issue.

I urge you to get in touch with your Senators and Congressman to voice your opinion in favor of the Federal Marriage Amendment. Too much is at stake. We will not recognize this country in a few years if this issue goes unchallenged.

What's Wrong with Same-Sex Marriage?

Matt Daniels has this to say about this amendment and how critical it is to pass it:

> Many of the elites in our nation, which include the courts and these groups that have access to the courts, have decided that marriage as a man and a woman should be destroyed. There is no evidence in favor of the benefits of destroying marriage, quite to the contrary, all of the evidence shows the sexual revolution has been a disaster. By the way, the forces that were responsible for the sexual revolution, they should be apologizing now to America for 30 years of devastation, of child poverty, of kids being born out of wedlock, ending up on welfare, ending up in prison; they should be apologizing for that, but they're not, they're trying to push it to the next level and actually take away the legal road map to marriage and the family which would be devastating for children, and they're doing it through the courts. It's a profoundly destructive social revolution and it's also anti-democratic because the American people don't want it.[7]

On Black Monday, May 17, 2004, when homosexuals "married" each other in Massachusetts, Tony Perkins, president of the Family Research Council, issued a statement:

> The so-called "gay agenda" is far-reaching, and it encompasses much more than the fight for marriage rights. If we do not immediately pass a Constitutional amendment protecting marriage, we will not only lose the institution of marriage in our nation, but eventually all critics of the homosexual lifestyle will be silenced. Churches will be muted, schools will be forced to promote homosexuality as a consequence-free alternative lifestyle, and our nation will find itself embroiled in a cultural, legal and moral quagmire.[8]

Conclusion

America, take your pick. Marriage between one man and one woman, as God intended, or the floodgates opened up by societal acceptance of same-sex marriage. The choice is ours. God and nature or a panoply of bad outcomes that will follow the state's stamp of approval on same-sex marriage. Forty years after the sexual revolution promised "free love" but brought divorce, illegitimacy, STDs, fatherlessness, and abortion, the last thing our nation needs is one more misguided social experiment. The Supreme Court once called marriage and the family the "sure foundation of all that is stable and noble in our civilization." If we monkey with that foundation, expect wrenching devastation to follow. May God help us as a nation to repent and fix this thing before it's too late.

Soli Deo Gloria.

Notes

Chapter One
The Importance of Marriage

1. *The New York Times,* November 23, 2003, quoted in Phyllis Schlafly, *Phyllis Schlafly Report* (Alton, IL: Eagle Forum, December 2003), 2.
2. James Dobson, "Family News from Dr. James Dobson," Colorado Springs: Focus on the Family, September 2003, 4.
3. Linda J. Waite and Maggie Gallagher, *The Case for Marriage: Why Married People Are Happier, Healthier, and Better Off Financially* (New York: Doubleday, 2000), 67, 148.
4. Ibid., 186.
5. Barbara Dafoe Whitehead, *The Divorce Culture* (New York: Alfred A. Knopf, 1997), 188-189.
6. Betty Friedan, *The Feminine Mystique* (New York: Dell, 1963/1977), 294.
7. Remarks of Rosie O'Donnell on *Good Morning America,* ABC-TV, February 26, 2004.
8. Maria Xiridou, Ronald Geskus, Jon DeWit, Roel Coutinho, and Mirjam Kretzschmar, "The Contribution of Steady and Casual Partnerships to the Incidence of HIV Infection Among Homosexual Men in Amsterdam," *AIDS,* 17 (2003): 1029-1038.
9. Amy Fagan, "Study Finds Gay Unions Brief," *The Washington Times,* July 11, 2003.
10. Robert T. Michael, John H. Gagnon, Edward O. Laumann, and Gina Kolata, *Sex in America: A Definitive Survey* (Boston: Little, Brown and Company, 1994), 124.
11. Ibid., 112, 119, 124-125.
12. Ibid., 89.

Chapter Two
The Real Reason for the Push for Same-Sex Marriage

1. Josh McDowell and Bob Hostetler, *The New Tolerance* (Wheaton, IL: Tyndale House, 1998), 32.
2. Andrew Sullivan, *Virtually Normal* (New York: Alfred A. Knopf, 1995), quoted in Richard Bastien, "The Impact of Same-sex Unions," July/August 2003, http://www.catholicinsight.com/original/political/homo/impactofsame_0703.html
3. Michelangelo Signorile, "Bridal Wave," *OUT* magazine, December/January 1994, 161.
4. Michelangelo Signorile, "I Do, I Do, I Do, I Do, I Do," *OUT* magazine, May 1996, 30.
5. Timothy J. Dailey, Ph.D., "Comparing the Lifestyles of Homosexual Couples to Married Couples," Washington, DC: Family Research Council, April 11, 2004, 7.

6. Phyllis Schlafly, *Phyllis Schlafly Report,* Alton, IL: Eagle Forum, December 2003, 2.
7. John D'Emilio, board member of the National Gay and Lesbian Task Force, "The Irresistible Force of Gay Power," 1993, quoted in *NARTH Bulletin,* December 1994, Volume 2, Number 3, 2.
8. "Death of a Myth," *NARTH Bulletin,* Volume 1, Number 3, July 1993, 3. See also "1% in Study Say They're Homosexual," Ft. Lauderdale: *Sun-Sentinel,* April 15, 1993.
9. "Death of a Myth," *NARTH Bulletin,* July 1993, 1.
10. "Ex-Gay Man Appreciates Encouragement," *NARTH Bulletin,* Volume 2, Number 1, March 1994, 6.
11. Robert T. Michael, John H. Gagnon, Edward O. Laumann, and Gina Kolata, *Sex in America: A Definitive Survey* (Boston: Little, Brown and Company, 1994), 176.
12. Transcript of an interview with Matthew Daniels, Ft. Lauderdale: Coral Ridge Ministries-TV, on location in Northern Virginia, May 2003.
13. Transcript from an interview with Kerby Anderson, Ft. Lauderdale: Coral Ridge Ministries-TV, on location in Charlotte, NC, February 2004.
14. Ibid.
15. The Christian Law Association, based in Seminole, Florida, receives on average more than 75,000 first-time phone calls from people needing their help. They do not charge these people, as what they do is a ministry of helps. This statistic shows how in trouble our religious freedoms are now. Imagine if same-sex marriage becomes fully legal everywhere. We could lose religious liberty in our lifetime. Yet America was settled and founded for the most part by Christians seeking religious liberty.
16. Transcript from an interview of David Gibbs III, Ft. Lauderdale: Coral Ridge Ministries-TV, February 2004.
17. U.S. Constitution, Article IV, Section 1.
18. Transcript from an interview with Matthew Daniels.
19. Marshall Kirk and Hunter Madsen, *After the Ball: How America Will Conquer Its Fear and Hatred of Gays in the 90s* (New York: Doubleday, 1989), quoted in "Selling 'Gay' to Straight America," *NARTH Bulletin,* Volume 1, Number 3, July 1993, 3.
20. The entire last chapter of this book is devoted to testimonials of former homosexuals and lesbians who have changed through the power of Jesus Christ.
21. Transcript of an interview with Matthew Daniels.
22. Ibid.
23. Ibid.

Chapter Three
Intolerance

1. Josh McDowell and Bob Hostetler, *The New Tolerance* (Wheaton, IL: Tyndale House, 1998), 26-27.
2. This occurred on a Sunday night in September 1993 at Hamilton Square Baptist Church, San Francisco. Rev. David Innis is the pastor. The incident was sparked by the fact that Rev. Lou Sheldon, a Presbyterian minister and profamily Christian activist, was going to speak at the church that night.

3. Chuck Donovan, Letter from Family Research Council, Washington, DC, July 14, 2000.
4. Observation of Stephen Bates in McDowell and Hostetler, *The New Tolerance*, 111.
5. Kenneth Stern in ibid.
6. S. Robert Lichter, Linda S. Lichter, and Stanley Rothman, with the assistance of Daniel Amundson, *Prime Time: How TV Portrays American Culture* (Washington, DC: Regnery, 1994), 422-424.
7. "Leaders Decry Rising Hostility to Christians," *The Los Angeles Times*, September 19, 1999, A08.
8. Letter from Cal Thomas to Jerry Newcombe, April 15, 1995.

Chapter Four
The Top Twelve Reasons We're Opposed to
Same-Sex Marriage

1. Transcript for an interview with Matt Daniels of the Alliance for Marriage. Ft. Lauderdale: Coral Ridge Ministries-TV, May 2003.
2. "A Cross-Cultural Perspective," *NARTH Bulletin*, Volume 1, Number 4, November 1993, 5.
3. Warren Burger, quoted in Dr. Charles Socarides, *Homosexuality: A Freedom Too Far* (Phoenix: Adam Margrave Books, 1995), 49.
4. Transcript for an interview with Matt Daniels.
5. Chuck Colson in pre-recorded remarks made during a special, live teleconference sponsored by Family Research Council, held in Colorado Springs and shown live in more than 500 churches nationwide, May 23, 2004.
6. Transcript of an interview with Anthony Falzarano on location in Washington, DC, Ft. Lauderdale, FL: Coral Ridge Ministries-TV, August 19, 1998.
7. Transcript of an interview with Craig Parshall for Ft. Lauderdale: Coral Ridge Ministries-TV, on location in Charlotte, NC, February 2004.
8. Transcript from an interview with Genevieve Wood for Ft. Lauderdale, FL: *The Coral Ridge Hour*, on location in Washington, DC, May 2004.
9. Stanley Kurtz, "Death of Marriage in Scandinavia," *The Boston Globe*, March 10, 2004.
10. Transcript from an interview with Craig Parshall.
11. Ibid.
12. Ibid.
13. Transcript of an interview with Bob Knight on location in Bradenton, FL, Ft. Lauderdale, FL: Coral Ridge Ministries-TV, January 1997.
14. Transcript from an interview with Craig Parshall.
15. Ibid.
16. Transcript of an interview with Matt Daniels.
17. Governor Mitt Romney, *The Wall Street Journal*, February 5, 2004.
18. Michael Kinsley, "Abolish Marriage: Let's Really Get the Government Out of Our Bedrooms," *Washington Post*, July 3, 2003, A23.
19. Transcript of an interview with Craig Parshall.
20. Transcript of an interview with Matt Daniels.
21. Transcript of an interview with Bob Knight.
22. Lynn Vincent, "Remaining Silent," *World*, May 8, 2004, 33.

23. Ibid.
24. Mary Ann Glendon, "For Better or for Worse?" *The Wall Street Journal*, February 25, 2004.

Chapter Five
Entertaining Angels Unawares

1. Henry H. Halley, *Halley's Bible Handbook* (Grand Rapids, MI: Zondervan Publishing House, 1965), 98.
2. Who coined the word *homosexuality*? Dr. Charles Socarides, a psychiatrist and the author of *Homosexuality: A Freedom Too Far*, says that "K. M. Benkert, writing in Germany under the pseudonym of Kertbeny" created the term *Homosexualitat* in 1869. The word "made its way into English two decades later" (Phoenix: Adam Margrave Books, 1995), 15.
3. Please note that Christian scholars do not believe the death penalty is to be applied today for homosexuality or for many of the offenses listed in the Old Testament—with the exception of murder (Gen. 9:6). There are three types of law in the Old Testament. There were, first of all, the *civil laws*. These were the laws for the nation of Israel, which was a theocracy ruled by God, who was the only Lawgiver in Zion. There was no parliament or congress in Israel to pass laws. God gave them all of the laws they had. Those laws (the civil laws) have disappeared with the disappearance of the theocratic state of Israel in A.D. 70. You can detect the civil laws by the fact that they have attached to them temporal penalties, such as fines or stripes or death. Second, there were the *ceremonial laws*, which prefigured and foreshadowed the coming of Jesus Christ as the Messiah. These were the shadows, and when the substance appeared, the shadows fell away; so those ceremonial laws are now gone. The sin offering and the trespass offering and all such ceremonial laws as that are pointing toward a religious object: the coming of the Messiah. But there remains the third part of the law given by God at Sinai: the *moral law*, which is a reflection of the eternal and holy nature of God. This is eternal and immutable. This has never passed away and will never pass away. It is the very Law of the Living God for His moral creatures. The moral laws are best summed up in the Ten Commandments.
4. Rev. Elder Donald Eastman, *Homosexuality: Not a Sin, Not a Sickness* (Los Angeles: Universal Fellowship of Metropolitan Community Churches, 1990), 4.
5. See *American Scholar,* Winter 1993, 17-30.
6. Charles Krauthammer, *New Republic,* November 22, 1993, 20-25, quoted in *NARTH Bulletin,* Volume 2, Number 1, March 1994, 4-5.
7. Quoted in *NARTH Bulletin,* Volume 1, Number 3, July 1993, 7.

Chapter Six
Homosexuality's Deadly Lifestyle

1. Paul Cameron, in "Coming Out: Breaking Free from Homosexuality," Ft. Lauderdale, FL: Coral Ridge Ministries-TV, October 11, 1998.
2. Ibid.
3. Transcript of an interview with Bill Bennett on location in Washington, DC, Ft. Lauderdale: Coral Ridge Ministries-TV, January 1998.
4. Ibid.
5. Remarks of an ex-gay, in "Coming Out: Breaking Free from Homosexuality."
6. *Miami Herald,* April 1, 1993.

7. Laura Meckler, AP Writer, "Satcher Urges Respect on Sex Values," *Washington Post,* June 28, 2001. http://www.washingtonpost.com
8. Peter Sprigg and Timothy Dailey, *Getting It Straight: What the Research Shows About Homosexuality* (Washington, DC: Family Research Council, 2004), 71.
9. Lorraine Day, M.D., *AIDS: What the Government Isn't Telling You* (Palm Desert, CA: Rockford Press, 1991), 122.
10. Ibid., 123.
11. Ibid., 111.
12. Remarks of Dr. Stanley Monteith, in "Coming Out: Breaking Free from Homosexuality."
13. Remarks of Bob Knight in ibid.
14. "Abstract 418 from the 2002 National STD Prevention Conference, 'Patterns of STD Infection, HIV Coinfection, and Risk-Behavior among MSM at a Boston Community Health Center,'" National Center for HIV, STD and TB Prevention, Division of Sexually Transmitted Diseases (March 5, 2002).
15. Sprigg and Dailey, *Getting It Straight,* 76.
16. Bill Roundy, "STDs Up Among Gay Men: CDC Says Rise Is Due to HIV Misperceptions," quoted in Sprigg and Dailey, *Getting It Straight,* 76.
17. Remarks of Dave Foster, in "Coming Out: Breaking Free from Homosexuality."
18. Remarks of an ex-gay, in ibid.
19. Michelangelo Signorile, *Life Outside* (New York: HarperCollins, 1997), 33.
20. Ibid., 75-76.
21. Remarks of Paul Cameron, in "Coming Out: Breaking Free from Homosexuality." See also S. Holt, "Ending the Cycle of Domestic Violence," *Gay & Lesbian Times,* September 26, 1996, 39.
22. Remarks of Dave Foster, in "Coming Out: Breaking Free from Homosexuality."
23. Remarks of an ex-gay, in ibid.
24. Remarks of Bob Knight, in ibid.
25. Signorile, *Life Outside,* 127.
26. Remarks of Mark Culligan, in "Coming Out: Breaking Free from Homosexuality."
27. Remarks of Dave Foster, in ibid.

Chapter Seven
Scientific Reasons Why Homosexuals Aren't Born That Way

1. Peter Sprigg and Timothy Dailey, *Getting It Straight: What the Research Shows About Homosexuality* (Washington, DC: Family Research Council, 2004), vi-vii.
2. Ibid., 2.
3. Ibid., 3.
4. Dr. Charles Socarides, *Homosexuality: A Freedom Too Far* (Phoenix: Adam Margrave Books, 1995), 93.
5. Miron Baron, "Genetic Linkage and Male Homosexual Orientation," *BMJ (British Medical Journal),* August 7, 1993, 307:337.
6. William Byne and Bruce Parsons, "Human Sexual Orientation: The Biologic Theories Reappraised," *Archives of General Psychiatry,* March 1993, 50:230, cited in Peter Sprigg and Timothy Dailey, *Getting It Straight: What the Research Shows About Homosexuality* (Washington, DC: Family Research Council, 2004), 9.
7. Socarides, *Homosexuality,* 96.

8. Ibid., 94.
9. Sprigg and Dailey, *Getting It Straight*, 13.
10. George Rice, Carol Anderson, Neil Risch, and George Ebers, "Male Homosexuality: Absence of Linkage to Microsatellite Markers at Xq28," *Science*, April 1999, 284:665.
11. Sprigg and Dailey, *Getting It Straight*, 16.
12. Byne and Parsons, "Human Sexual Orientation," 50:236.
13. See G. van den Aardweg, *On the Origins and Treatment of Homosexuality: A Psychoanalytic Reinterpretation* (Westport, CT: Praeger, 1986).
14. Dr. Richard Fitzgibbons, in "Coming Out: Breaking Free from Homosexuality," Ft. Lauderdale: Coral Ridge Ministries-TV, October 11, 1998.
15. Dr. James Mallory, in ibid.
16. Ibid.
17. Steven Goldberg, *When Wish Replaces Thought: Why So Much of What You Believe Is False* (Buffalo, NY: Prometheus Books, 1992), quoted in *NARTH Bulletin*, Volume 2, Number 3, December 1994, 5.
18. "Dr. Charles Silverstein: An Update on His Professional Contributions," *NARTH Bulletin*, Volume 2, Number 1, March 1994, 5.
19. Dr. Charles Socarides, in "Coming Out: Breaking Free from Homosexuality."
20. Dr. Charles Socarides, *Homosexuality*, 74.
21. Dr. James Mallory, in "Coming Out: Breaking Free from Homosexuality."
22. Dr. Charles Socarides, in ibid.
23. Based on a report in *Psychiatric News*, September 3, 1993, paraphrased in "U.S. Psychiatrists' View on Homosexuality Differs from Colleagues in Foreign Countries," *NARTH Bulletin*, November 1993, Volume 1, Number 4, 6.
24. Dr. Charles Socarides, in "Coming Out: Breaking Free from Homosexuality."
25. Dr. James Mallory, in ibid.
26. Dr. Richard Fitzgibbons, in ibid.
27. Dr. Charles Socarides, in ibid.
28. Dr. Richard Fitzgibbons, in ibid.
29. Dr. Joseph Nicolosi, *Reparative Therapy of Male Homosexuality* (Northvale, NJ: Jason Aronson, 1991).
30. Dr. Joseph Nicolosi, in "Coming Out: Breaking Free from Homosexuality."
31. Ibid.
32. Marvin Siegelman, "Parental Background of Male Homosexuals and Heterosexuals," *Archives of Sexual Behavior*, 3 (1974): 3-4.
33. Daniel G. Brown, "Homosexuality and Family Dynamics," *Bulletin of the Menninger Clinic* 27 (5):232 (September 1963), in Sprigg and Dailey, *Getting It Straight*, 26.
34. Dr. Charles Socarides, *Homosexuality*, 87.
35. Jeff Johnson, in "Coming Out: Breaking Free from Homosexuality."

Chapter Eight
Confessions of Ex-gays and Ex-lesbians

1. Sy Rogers, "The Man in the Mirror," Linsdale, TX: *The Last Days Magazine*, 1980, 1983, 1991. Reprinted as an Exodus International tract by the same title, 2.
2. The confessions of ex-gays in this chapter are largely based on a television segment

produced by Jerry Newcombe for D. James Kennedy, *The Coral Ridge Hour,* April 1997. (Minor verbal stumbles—e.g., uhs, ers, you knows—have been removed.)

3. Remarks of Thom Rogers, in "AIDS: Anatomy of a Crisis," Ft. Lauderdale: Coral Ridge Ministries-TV, July 1988.
4. Remarks of Van Craig, in ibid.
5. Ibid.
6. Remarks of Josh McDowell, in ibid.
7. Remarks of Dr. Elizabeth Moberly, in ibid.
8. Ibid.
9. Ibid.
10. Ibid.

Epilogue
Where Do We Go from Here?

1. Canada is ahead of us in passing laws that make speaking out against homosexuality a hate crime. Because of their Human Rights Code, Hugh Owens of Regina, Saskatchewan and the newspaper *Saskatoon StarPhoenix* were fined and forced to pay $4,500 damages to three homosexual men whom they offended. Their offense? Owens designed an ad, which the paper published, listing four Bible references—not the verses themselves, only their addresses. On the left side, it simply said:

Romans 1
Leviticus 18:22
Leviticus 20:13
1 Corinthians 6:9-10

On the right side it had the equal sign plus a stick figure drawing of two men holding hands in a circle with a slash through it (like the no U-turn signs). Higher courts upheld this sentence. To make matters worse, Canada added "sexual orientation" to their hate crimes bill in April 2004. What happened to Owens and the *Saskatoon StarPhoenix* could be a chilling foretaste of what is to come here if same-sex marriage gets fully accepted. Source: Art Moore, "Bible Verses Regarded as Hate Literature," *WorldNetDaily,* February 18, 2003.
2. Transcript from an interview with Rev. Ingo Sünderland on location in Gottenberg, Sweden. Ft. Lauderdale: Coral Ridge Ministries-TV, July 2003.
3. Ibid.
4. David Crary, "Coalition Proposes Amending Constitution to Block Gay Marriage," Associated Press, July 10, 2001.
5. *Casey v. Planned Parenthood,* U.S. Supreme Court decision of 1992, which upheld the pro-abortion rights position of *Roe v. Wade.*
6. Justice Anthony Kennedy for the majority of the U.S. Supreme Court, *Lawrence v. Texas,* June 2003.
7. Transcript from an interview with Matt Daniels for *The Coral Ridge Hour,* Ft. Lauderdale: Coral Ridge Ministries-TV, May 2003.
8. Tony Perkins, "FRC Statement on Massachusetts Homosexual 'Marriages'" (Washington, DC: Family Research Council, May 17, 2004).

Index